Providing Quality Service

Providing Quality Service

What Every Hospitality Service Provider Needs to Know

William B. Martin, Ph.D.
The Collins School of Hospitality Management
California State Polytechnic University, Pomona

Prentice Hall

Upper Saddle River, New Jersey 07458

Library of Congress Cataloging-in-Publication Data

Martin, William B.
  Providing quality service : what every hospitality service provider
needs to know / William B. Martin.
    p. cm.
    Includes bibliographical references and index.
    ISBN 0-13-096745-9
  1. Hospitality industry. I. Title.
    TX911 .M372 2003
    647.94--dc21

                                                2002004228

Executive Editor: Vern Anthony
Associate Editor: Marion Gottlieb
Production Editor: Russell Jones, Pine Tree
   Composition, Inc.
Production Liaison: Adele M. Kupchik
**Director of Manufacturing
   and Production:** Bruce Johnson
Managing Editor: Mary Carnis
Manufacturing Buyer: Cathleen Petersen
Art Director: Cheryl Asherman
Cover Design Coordinator: Christopher Weigand
Cover Design: Kevin Kall
Marketing Manager: Ryan DeGrote
Editorial Assistant: Ann Brunner
Composition: Pine Tree Composition, Inc.
Printing and Binding: Von Hoffman Press, Inc.
Cover Printer: Coral Graphics

Prentice-Hall International (UK) Limited, *London*
Prentice-Hall of Australia Pty. Limited, *Sydney*
Prentice-Hall Canada Inc., *Toronto*
Prentice-Hall Hispanoamericana, S.A., *Mexico*
Prentice-Hall of India Private Limited, *New Delhi*
Prentice-Hall of Japan, Inc., *Tokyo*
Prentice-Hall Singapore Pte. Ltd.
Editora Prentice-Hall do Brasil, Ltda., *Rio de Janeiro*

10 9 8 7 6 5 4 3 2 1
ISBN 0-13-096745-9

To all of my children and stepchildren who have been, are, and will be hospitality service providers and from whom I continually learn.

Mindy

Scott

Cassie

Will

Josie

Christen

Courtney

Contents

Application Interaction Exercises

Figures

xiii

Preface

This textbook serves as a companion to *Quality Service—What Every Hospitality Manager Needs to Know*. The focus of that book is on how management is the key to delivering quality service in hospitality organizations. It emphasizes that for quality service to occur, it must be well managed. That simple fact remains as true as ever. If that is so, you may ask, why bother with a service book addressed to hospitality service providers? The answer lies in the very nature of customer service. Managers do play a vital and integral role in the delivery of customer service. Over the long haul, what they do makes or breaks the level of service provided throughout the organization. They establish the climate and service standards, do the hiring, conduct training, provide performance feedback, and reward successes. Yet, in spite of this critical managerial role, it is the service provider who ultimately delivers the actual service.

At the point of each and every service encounter with each and every customer, it is the service provider who is in control, not management. The service provider greets the guest, communicates with the guest, renders the necessary service, interacts with the guest in a variety of ways, completes the transaction, and sends the guest on his or her way. In most hospitality operations, this encounter occurs without a manager being close by or, sometimes, even available. Given this scenario, virtually all hospitality service providers are in a situation where they can make choices about what to do, say and act. The fact of the matter is, with or without managerial support, service providers can determine, to a great extent, the success of each and every customer service encounter. They can choose to provide quality customer service or not—assuming they understand what quality customer service is all about. Unfortunately, however, too many hospitality service providers do not fully comprehend what quality customer service is all about. They are thrown into the job with minimal customer service preparation or training. It is no surprise that delivering quality service remains the single biggest challenge in the hospitality industry today.

This book confronts that challenge head-on. It serves as a complete guide to success for an existing or potential hospitality service provider. Whatever the position, whatever the nature of the operation, if it's hospitality and the position requires interaction with guests in any way, this book outlines a comprehensive quality customer service action plan for that position. It covers the full spectrum of quality service—what it is and how to provide it.

When it comes to hospitality, the proof of the pudding is in the doing. That is why this book includes thirty-two **application interaction exercises**. They have been created so that the reader may take the concepts and suggestions from the book and apply them to specific hospitality settings. They also serve as a useful introduction to more hands-on, on-the-job training. Nonetheless, this book is not intended to replace on-the-job training; it is designed to supplement and strengthen it.

The flexibility of this book facilitates its use in an ongoing hospitality operation and in an academic setting. In either environment the reviews and exercises at the end of each chapter set the stage for lively discussion and enthusiastic learning. Instructors, trainers, and learners alike will have fun with them. The book can be used in any hospitality classroom or training session that covers the principles of customer service.

The purpose of this book is to generate success: success for hospitality service providers, success for teachers and trainers, success for hospitality operations, and success for all their customers. Everybody can end up winning. But such success doesn't just happen. There are principles, methods, and skills that must be mastered. And mastery requires some effort, time, and practice. This book points the way. More important, it helps make winning at customer service happen. My intention in writing this book is that the journey of learning the knowledge and skills required of a quality hospitality service provider is enjoyable as well as rewarding. I trust that it will be.

William B. Martin
Pomona, California

Acknowledgments

To Vern Anthony of Prentice-Hall, Inc.
   For your foresight in first suggesting this project.

To Marion Gottlieb of Prentice-Hall, Inc.
   For your continuing support and keeping me on track during the writing phase of this volume and its complementary instructor's manual.

To Mike Crisp of Crisp Publications, Inc.
   For your professional courtesy in allowing me to use several exercises and ideas from my book *Quality Customer Service* in this volume.

To Russell Jones and the staff of Pine Tree Composition, Inc.
   For your editing and creative prowess in putting this volume together in a readable and user-friendly format.

To all the Hospitality Service Provider Winners I have used as examples in this volume
   For your meritorious Hall of Fame performances.

Providing Quality Service

Section I

CUSTOMER SERVICE FUNDAMENTALS—

Providing Hospitality at Its Best

1

Winning with the Customer

Why should you read this book? After all, you probably know "good" service when you see it. Whether you have been a customer, client, patient, guest, or member, you have most likely been the recipient of service at numerous restaurants, hotels, supermarkets, banks, health care facilities, retail stores, and so on. You know how you like to be treated as a customer. You know what it is like to be a receiver of customer service—both good and bad. But now, you have become or are considering becoming a service provider yourself. This is a whole new world. The tables have been turned. It is now your turn to deliver service rather than receive it. You have entered or are about to enter the world of the *hospitality service provider*.

You may be a host/hostess in a restaurant, a counter person in a quick food service operation, a service associate at the front desk of a hotel, or a restaurant food server. You may work in a theme park, a country club, an athletic club, or in a travel-related business. But whatever hospitality environment you may be working in or considering, you will interact with customers in one way or another. What does this mean? How can you be successful? How can you make sure the customers' experiences are of quality? And how can you make sure *your* experience is a quality one as well?

A Win-Win Situation

The premise of this book is quite simple: *For quality service to occur, both the customer and the service provider must win.* This means the customer wins and you win. When you both win, we can truly refer to the level of service as one of quality. This means that the customer should not win at your expense, and that you should not win at the customer's expense. (Both of these situations can happen, but when they do, quality service is not happening.) Quality service requires a win-win encounter between the service provider and the customer. This is what I call "winning with the customer."

R equired Focus

The second point of this book is that quality service doesn't just happen. It is not a matter of luck, chance, or good vibrations. Quality service requires certain, specific actions—actions initiated by you which, in turn, generate specific actions from your customers. Even though winning with the customer may be simple to comprehend, that does not mean that it is easy to accomplish. In fact, delivering quality service in a fasted-paced, high-pressured hospitality environment day-in and day-out is quite challenging. Moreover, delivering service at a level of quality that wows the customer does not just happen. In other words, quality service doesn't automatically occur once you are hired as a service provider. There are some basic concepts to understand and a variety of techniques to master. In addition, you don't provide quality service merely by being a smart or talented individual. That helps, of course, but many smart and talented individuals have failed at delivering quality customer service. Many of these failures, I believe, are due to a misunderstanding of what quality service is all about. If you are going to be successful at customer service what is required first and foremost is a willingness to learn and a desire to be a successful service provider. If you have that and follow the contents of this book, success will come. You not only will understand what it takes to be successful but also you will be able to carry it out—to do it. This means that you will have mastered the skills for creating a win-win relationship with your customers.

Quality Service Must Be a Job Priority

Unfortunately, in the hospitality industry as a whole, delivering quality customer service often plays second fiddle to delivering quality food and rooms. Of course, a great meal and a welcoming guest room don't just happen either. A lot of time and effort must go into making sure these products meet not only organizational expectations but also those of the customer. Not only that, they also require a significant amount of time and energy each and every day because these products represent the very heart of the hospitality business. *However, the same is true for quality service.* Most experienced hospitality service providers would not openly deny this. They are good at extolling the virtues and importance of quality service. They know, in their hearts and minds, how vital it is. But, that does not necessarily mean that they are *doing* all the right things to make it happen. In fact, my experience tells me that most hospitality service providers, though good at providing lip service on behalf of quality service, spend less time than they think actually delivering it. Moreover, most of them are not even aware of what they can and should do to render it more effectively.

So, why should you read this book? If you hold a service provider position somewhere within the hospitality industry, or plan to be a service provider some time in the future, this book will tell you everything you need to know about transforming everyday hum-drum service into a quality of customer service that others will rave about. And when that happens, you will have experienced your own hospitality customer service success story. After you have translated the principles outlined in this book into your everyday service actions, you will most assuredly receive the many joys and rewards of becoming a *hospitality service provider winner.*

Chapter 1 in Review

KEY CONCEPTS

1. For quality customer service to occur, both the customer and the service provider must win.

2. Quality service requires certain specific actions from the service provider.

3. Success at customer service comes from a willingness to learn, a desire to be successful, and making quality service a job priority.

KEY TERM

Win-win situation

STUDY QUESTIONS/DISCUSSION STIMULATORS

1. What insight does experience being a customer provide a person considering becoming a service provider?

2. Why is quality service important to the hospitality industry?

3. Why is it important for both the customer and the service provider to win as a result of a customer service encounter?

4. Why is providing customer service often mistakenly perceived by some as an easy job?

5. Why do many hospitality organizations concentrate more on the quality of food and rooms than on quality service?

6. What do you want to personally accomplish by reading this book?

APPLICATION INTERACTION EXERCISE 1

WINNING WITH THE CUSTOMER

1. Can you describe a customer service situation that you have experienced or observed where both the customer and the service provider ended up winning? What happened? Why were both parties winners?

_____

_____

_____

2. Can you describe a customer service situation that you experienced or observed where the customer won at the expense of the service provider? This is a win-lose situation where the customer ends up winning but the service provider ends up losing. What happened? How did the service provider respond? Why should these situations be avoided?

_____

_____

_____

3. Can you describe a customer service situation that you experienced or observed where the customer lost at the expense of the service provider? In this case, the customer ends up losing, while the service provider wins. What happened? Why should these situations be avoided?

_____

_____

_____

4. Can you describe a customer service situation that you experienced or observed where both the customer and service provider ended up losing? This is called a lose-lose interaction. What happened? Why should these situations be avoided?

_____

_____

_____

APPLICATION INTERACTION EXERCISE 2

FOCUSING ON QUALITY SERVICE

1. What does the phrase, "focusing on quality service" mean to you?

_____

_____

_____

How does it apply to your ability to deliver quality customer service?

_____

_____

_____

2. Are YOU ready to become a service provider winner? _____

(If you can answer "yes" to the following questions, you are most likely ready.)

	Yes	No
A. Are you genuinely enthusiastic about being a service provider?	_____	_____
B. Are you generally open to new experiences?	_____	_____
C. Are you willing to learn new or different ways of doing a job you are currently or have previously performed?	_____	_____
D. Do you believe there are still some things you can learn that will make you a better service provider?	_____	_____
E. Do you genuinely enjoy working with and for other people?	_____	_____
F. Do you have the ability to make the customer feel important?	_____	_____
G. Do you have a high energy level and enjoy a fast pace of work?	_____	_____
H. Are you flexible and adaptable to new demands and experiences?	_____	_____

APPLICATION INTERACTION EXERCISE 3

SERVICE SKILLS INVENTORY

This self-rating scale will help identify those service areas that you may need to learn more about to improve your service provider skills. Place a check in the appropriate column.

	Know nothing Need to learn all I can	Know a little Need to learn more	Know quite a bit Need to brush up	Know all there is to know
ABILITY TO—				
1. Provide timely service	_____	_____	_____	_____
2. Be flexible and accommodating to customer needs	_____	_____	_____	_____
3. Anticipate customer needs in advance	_____	_____	_____	_____
4. Use effective communication skills	_____	_____	_____	_____
5. Solicit feedback from customers	_____	_____	_____	_____
6. Be well organized getting the job done	_____	_____	_____	_____
7. Show a positive attitude when the going gets tough	_____	_____	_____	_____
8. Convey positive body language	_____	_____	_____	_____
9. Tune-in to the special needs of customers	_____	_____	_____	_____
10. Provide help and assistance to guests	_____	_____	_____	_____
11. Use appropriate language at all times	_____	_____	_____	_____
12. Speak in a friendly, hospitable tone of voice	_____	_____	_____	_____
13. Be an effective salesperson	_____	_____	_____	_____
14. Handle difficult customers in a gracious, constructive way	_____	_____	_____	_____

2

The Nature
of Customer Service

What Is Customer Service Anyway?

The perception of what exactly customer service is may vary from one person to the next, depending on an individual's experience as a customer or on one's work experience. As participants in today's world, everyday life thrusts us into numerous customer service encounters. Whether it is an irritating sales call that comes right at the dinner hour, our interaction with the grocery store clerk, the bank teller, the hardware store assistant, or the fast-food counter person, most of us are seasoned veterans of customer service interactions—just from being a customer. When asked to define customer service from a customer's perspective, many of us might say something like:

"Customer service means taking care of me."

"Customer service is being greeted with a smile."

"I call customer service when I have a problem."

"Customer service is talking to a real person rather than a computer."

"Customer service means getting my order right, the first time."

These responses are colored by the breadth and depth of various customer service experiences each of us may have had as a recipient of service. On the other hand, if you have already had experience as a provider of service in a restaurant, a hotel, a club, a travel-related business, or other sales organization, you might define customer service somewhat differently. Here are a few possibilities:

"Customer service is being as fast as I can be."

"Customer service is being nice to guests."

"Customer service is just doing my job."

"Customer service is getting that customer to smile back."

"Customer service is making the sale."

"Customer service is helping and then helping some more."

Why all these different responses? Why do some people see customer service in one way and other people see it quite differently? Which ones are right? The answer is they are all right. Why is this so? Why does the nature of customer service appear to be so illusive? One reason is customer service is *intangible*. Unlike a meal on a plate or a room at an inn, it cannot be directly measured, weighed, inspected, touched, or smelled. That is why we need to take a closer look at it. To help us in this process, we need to—

1. Understand the difference between tangible and intangible products, and

2. Understand the special status of the customer in all of this.

Tangibles vs. Intangibles

Customer service is different from other hospitality products. It is different because it is intangible. And, because it is intangible, it creates a major service provider challenge. Most of us in the hospitality industry understand and appreciate the fact that food service and lodging establishments are unique enterprises. Restaurants and hotels not only produce a product and sell it, but also handle the distribution and facilitate the consumption of the product. Moreover, in most cases, all the production processes are conducted under one roof, within one operation. But few of us in the hospitality business fully understand and appreciate the fact that outside the site of production—the kitchen or the guestroom—the operation's complexity multiplies geometrically. Too few of us really appreciate how much our intangible product—customer service—contributes to the overall success of the operation, particularly when it is compared with the tangible products of food and rooms.

Customer service reflects the people side of the hospitality business. If we fail to appreciate and understand the complexity of the people side, we are in trouble. But, in fact, many of us take it for granted. We get stuck in the "peas, potatoes, and pillows" side of the enterprise and hope that the people side, that illusive intangible part of what we do, will somehow take care of itself. Why does this happen? I think it happens because the tangibles are simply easier to deal with. Whether it is a guest room or a full meal on a plate, we can inspect it, touch it, even smell it to know whether the product is "right" or "wrong." Unfortunately, we can't do that with customer service. That makes delivering the people skills far more complex than delivering tangible products. Moreover, when service providers begin to interact with guests, people skills take on great importance to the operation's success. Because of their complexity and importance, people skills must not be left to chance in any hospitality organization. Whenever people skills are involved, we must consider the emotional, social, and cultural world of human needs, wants, expectations, rules, and ways of communicating. In short, all this is complicated stuff. Yet we cannot concentrate exclusively on the tangible side of hospitality enterprises just because it is easier to deal with. We must learn to deliver the intangible side, the people side, with all the energy and focus that we have traditionally given to the tangibles—that is, if we expect to provide quality customer service.

This book shows potential and current service providers how to develop a holistic view of quality customer service and come to appreciate not only how customers should be treated but also how this human dynamic can be brought to life in a hospitality operation. You can come to understand the importance of the human experience in addition to peas, potatoes, and pillows. By using the right actions and reinforcement, you can significantly improve your people skills. You can provide effective actions that make the service difference. In turn, the consumers of your hospitality products will get the kind of service they want, expect, and deserve. Both of you will end up winning.

The first step in doing this is adopting a customer service perspective.

Adopting a Customer Service Perspective

"The customer is king."

"The customer is the reason we exist."

"Without our customers we have nothing."

"Our customers define our business."

"If we don't understand our customers, we don't understand our business."

Each of these statements reflects a customer orientation—a view that the customer is vital to the nature and success of one's business. This is called a customer service perspective. Here are a few more.

"We are not providing quality service unless our customers say that we are."

"Our paychecks come from the customer."

"Customers are not an interruption of our work. They are the purpose of it."

"Customers are part of our business—not outsiders."

Adopting a customer service perspective requires us to look at hospitality organizations in a unique way. This view maintains that the most important activity in which the organization engages is the point in time when the organization's service provider interacts with the customer. In short, this is customer service's defining moment. This is the essence, the heart and soul, of customer service. This is the point of service encounter. This is what Jan Carlzon of Scandinavian Airlines has succinctly labeled, *The Moment of Truth.*

When the customer service encounter becomes the moment of truth for a hospitality organization, the entire focus of the organization is literally turned upside down as illustrated in Figure 2.1.

A front desk clerk, a restaurant food server, a housekeeper, a hotel sales and marketing professional, or a travel representative have hundreds of moments of truth each and every day. This makes every service provider critically important to the entire organization. The organization cannot succeed unless every service provider succeeds. Making sure that the moment of truth with the customer is a winning one is vital to everyone's success.

FIGURE 2.1

The Traditional Perspective

The Customer Service Perspective

Chapter 2 in Review

KEY CONCEPTS

1. Perception of what customer service is can vary from person to person, depending on life and work experiences.

2. Customer service is intangible and requires the same attention and focus as hospitality tangibles.

3. Adopting a customer service perspective requires us to look at hospitality organizations in a unique way represented by an inverted pyramid.

KEY TERMS

Customer service perspective
Intangibles
Moment of truth
Tangibles

STUDY QUESTIONS/DISCUSSION STIMULATORS

1. Why is it common for customers to define or describe customer service different from service providers?

2. How does customer service's intangibility make it more difficult to deliver than hospitality tangibles?

3. How are hospitality operations significantly different from typical nonhospitality operations?

4. What does the phrase "moment of truth" mean? Why is it important?

5. What is the difference between the traditional and the customer service perspective as depicted in Figure 2.1?

APPLICATION INTERACTION EXERCISE 4

HOW WOULD YOU DEFINE CUSTOMER SERVICE?

1. As a customer, guest, patient, or client, what does customer service mean to you?

_____

_____

_____

_____

_____

_____

2. As a service provider, or potential service provider, what does customer service mean to you?

_____

_____

_____

_____

_____

_____

3. What are the differences and/or similarities in your two responses?

_____

_____

_____

_____

_____

_____

APPLICATION INTERACTION EXERCISE 5

CUSTOMER SERVICE IS NOT LIKE A CAR

Customer service is *different from* a car because:

- You can't kick the tires.
- You can't open it up and sit inside.
- It doesn't come in optional colors.
- You can't keep it in your garage.
- You can't hear the sound of the engine.
- You can't even take it in for repair when it isn't working right.

Hospitality organizations deal in one way or another with tangible products or conditions. Like a car, these tangibles can be poked, prodded, weighed, or otherwise physically inspected. *Tangibles* often define the essence of what an organization is all about.

Some examples of hospitality tangibles are:

Computers	Germs	Guest rooms	Food
Equipment	Décor	Tickets	Airplanes
Uniforms	Buildings	Money	Furniture

1. If you are working in a hospitality organization, what are the major tangibles that you must deal with in your job?

   _____

   _____

   _____

2. What are the major tangibles that the organization, as a whole, considers to be most important?

   _____

   _____

   _____

APPLICATION INTERACTION EXERCISE 6

CUSTOMER SERVICE IS INTANGIBLE

Intangibles deal with the human side of hospitality. They include human emotions, behaviors, understandings, feelings, and perceptions.

Intangibles are often elusive because you can't inspect, touch, or smell them to know whether they are "right" or "wrong." However, like a tangible product, intangible customer service is often the key to hospitality success.

Some examples of customer service intangibles are:

Accommodation	Attentiveness	Attitude
Anticipation	Flow	Friendliness
Graciousness	Helpfulness	Knowledge
Satisfaction	Sensitivity	Tact
Tone	Understanding	Welcoming

What are some customer service intangibles that you have experienced?

As a customer?

_____

_____

_____

_____

As a service provider?

_____

_____

_____

_____

_____

_____

APPLICATION INTERACTION EXERCISE 7

THE CUSTOMER IS KING

"The customer is king."

"The customer is the reason we exist."

"Without our customers we have nothing."

"Our customers define our business."

"We are not providing quality service unless our customers think that we are."

"Our paychecks come from the customer."

"Customers are not an interruption of our work. They are the purpose of it."

"Customers are part of our business—not outsiders."

1. There are thousands of phrases that reflect a customer perspective. The ones listed reflect only a few of the many possibilities. Which one of these phrases strikes home for you? Why?

_____

_____

_____

_____

_____

2. If you were to create your own phrase reflecting a customer perspective, what would it say?

_____

_____

_____

_____

_____

_____

_____

APPLICATION INTERACTION EXERCISE 8

THE CUSTOMER SERVICE PERSPECTIVE

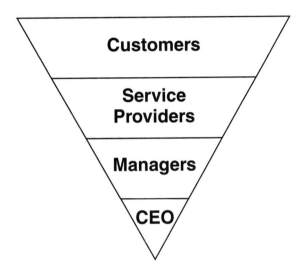

1. What does this inverted triangle say to you?

_____

_____

_____

2. What does this diagram say to you about the role of the service provider?

_____

_____

_____

3. What does this diagram say to you about the role of managers and executives?

_____

_____

_____

3

The Two Types
of Customers

■ ■ ■ ■ ■ ■ ■ ■ ■ ■ □ □

Who Are Your Customers?

Customers come in two varieties: external and internal.

EXTERNAL CUSTOMERS

External customers are those individuals who live and work outside, or apart from, the service providing organization. They come in many shapes, sizes, and varieties. There are long ones, short ones, skinny ones, and fat ones, light ones, dark ones, old ones, young ones, smart ones, and not-so-smart ones. There are first-time ones as well as repeat ones. You may even consider some of them old friends. There are ones who know what they want and ones who don't. Some arrive early, some late, some right on time. Most are nice, some are not. Some are understanding, some are not. Many speak your language, others do not. Yet each of these customers has two characteristics in common: They are the final targeted recipients of the service that a hospitality organization provides, *and* they are doing business with you because *they have chosen to.* They have made a conscious decision to seek service from you.

Most hospitality organizations target a defined group of customers. A targeted group of customers is part of what is commonly referred to as one's *market niche.* Quick-food service operators tend to target a different mix of customers than full-service restaurants. A resort hotel focuses on a distinct clientele compared with a downtown business hotel, and so forth. The point is, each hospitality organization has its own set of external customers with differing service needs, wants, and expectations. Developing a customer-service perspective requires that you are able to identify and deliver what it is that your customers expect. The bottom line is hospitality service providers cannot deliver quality customer service without first understanding the nature of what you are providing, and fully realizing what your external customers need and want.

Internal Customers

The second variety of customer is referred to as the *internal* customer. Internal customers are all the people *inside* the organization who are helped or otherwise impacted by the work of others within the organization. Internal customers, in contrast to external ones, may have little or no choice when it comes to receiving services, unless of course they decide to leave their job. No service work in any organization takes place in a vacuum. Everybody's work impacts one or more people, all the way from the top of the organization to the bottom. Furthermore, kitchen crew members provide service for catering and front-of-the-house food servers. Food servers, in turn, provide needed and vital service to the kitchen crew. Housekeeping departments in hotels have a similar mutual service relationship with the front desk as do flight crew and ground crew in the airline industry. Moreover, a CEO's service competency can have repercussions throughout the organization. It is important for all hospitality managers and service providers alike to understand and appreciate who exactly their internal customers are—those individuals and groups inside the organization to which service is provided, those people within the company who depend on your customer service competency.

Because of the need to serve internal as well as external customers, customer service must be *everybody's* job within a hospitality organization. The housekeeper cannot defer to the front desk.

The kitchen cannot think that customer service only occurs table-side. Moreover, management cannot divorce themselves either. They are part and parcel of the entire quality service chain of events. In fact, how management manages customer service and how service providers deliver it are the defining factors in this entire chain of mutual influence.

Chapter 3 in Review

KEY CONCEPTS

1. External customers are individuals who live and work outside of the hospitality organization and are doing business with you because they have chosen to do so.

2. Internal customers are people inside the organization who depend on you for service to accomplish their jobs.

3. Customer service is everybody's job within a hospitality organization.

KEY TERMS

External customers
Internal customers
Market niche

STUDY QUESTIONS/DISCUSSION STIMULATORS

1. What are the two key characteristics of external customers? Why are these characteristics important?

2. How is understanding an organization's market niche important? How does a particular market niche affect the level and types of service provided?

3. How are internal customers different from external ones? What is important about these differences?

4. Why is it important to understand the needs and wants of your internal customers?

APPLICATION INTERACTION EXERCISE 9

DEVELOPING A PROFILE OF YOUR *EXTERNAL* CUSTOMERS

1. Describe your *external* customers (age, gender, income, other characteristics).

_____

_____

_____

2. What is important to them?

_____

_____

_____

3. What do they like?

_____

_____

_____

4. What do they expect from you?

_____

_____

_____

5. How do they view you?

_____

_____

_____

6. What does this profile tell you about providing service to *external* customers?

_____

_____

_____

APPLICATION INTERACTION EXERCISE 10

DEVELOPING A PROFILE OF YOUR *INTERNAL* CUSTOMERS

1. Describe your *internal* customers (age, gender, income, other characteristics).

_____

_____

_____

2. What is important to them?

_____

_____

_____

3. What do they like?

_____

_____

_____

4. What do they expect from you?

_____

_____

_____

5. How do they view you?

_____

_____

_____

6. What does this profile tell you about providing service to *internal* customers?

_____

_____

_____

4

Defining "Quality" in Quality Service

What Is Quality Service?

We are now ready to address the question, what is *quality* customer service? So, here is my response.

Quality customer service is the ability to consistently meet external and internal customer needs, wants, and expectations involving procedural and personal encounters.

Okay, that's the definition. Now, an explanation is in order. Let's look at three of the key ingredients in this definition. First, there is the word "consistently." For customer service to receive a "quality" rating, it must be consistent. No service provider, of whom I am aware, delivers total quality customer service 100 percent of the time. The key to achieving quality customer service is to overwhelmingly increase the number of service encounter successes and significantly reduce the number of service failures—each and every day—to a point where service failures are few and far between. This is what I mean by consistent.

Second, quality customer service is based on *customer expectations*, not organizational needs. The focus must remain on the customer, internal as well as external. This means that quality service can only be described and understood from the customer's point of view. Meeting customer expectations may in fact make your job more challenging, if not more difficult. Yet quality customer service requires acceptance of this fact and a willingness to step up to the challenge.

Third, I have divided customer expectations into two service encounter dimensions: *procedural* and *personal*. The *procedural side* of service consists of the systems and processes used to deliver products and/or service. It is inherently mechanical in nature; the *personal side* of service encompasses how service providers use attitudes, behaviors, and verbal skills during the service encounter. In contrast to the procedural side, this side of service is inherently human in nature. In order for customer service to receive a "quality" rating, customer expectations in both the procedural and personal dimensions must be met.

The Four Customer Service Arenas

The procedural and personal dimensions of quality customer service can be represented in graphic form, as shown in Figure 4.1. In diagrams A–D, the vertical axis represents the degree of procedural service expected by the customer, and the horizontal axis reflects a measure of personal service expectations.

Four basic patterns of meeting customer expectations emerge. *Only one, diagram D, satisfies the definition of quality customer service.*

The freezer is a limited-service arena representing poor procedural and meager personal service. As shown in diagram A, the small size of this service arena leaves a great deal of room for improvement. In this case, service providers deliver inadequate procedural service that is hardly personal. Because service fails to meet timing and organization expectations, customers experience a great deal of inconvenience and frustration. Worse, service is generally insensitive to the customers' frustrations, conveying an attitude that is impersonal and aloof. Service providers

FIGURE 4.1

Diagram A: This reflects an operation that is low in both personal and procedural
The Freezer service. This "freezer" approach to service communicates to customers,
"We don't care."

Diagram B: This diagram represents proficient procedural service but a weakness in
The Factory the personal dimension. This "factory" approach to service communicates to
customers, "You are a number. We are here to process you."

Diagram C: The "friendly zoo" approach to service is very personal but lacks
The Friendly procedural consistency. This type of service communicates to customers,
Zoo "We are trying hard, but don't really know what we're doing."

Diagram D: This diagram represents Quality Customer Service. It is strong in
Quality both the personal and procedural dimensions. It communicates to
Customer customers, "We care, and we deliver."
Service

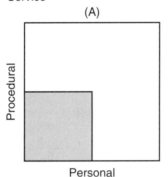

(A)

The **"Freezer"** service characteristics:

Procedural	**Personal**
Slow	Insensitive
Inconsistent	Cold or impersonal
Disorganized	Apathetic
Chaotic	Aloof
Inconvenient	Uninterested

Message to customers: **"We don't care."**

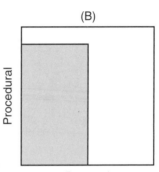

(B)

The **"Factory"** service characteristics:

Procedural	**Personal**
Timely	Insensitive
Efficient	Apathetic
Uniform	Aloof
	Uninterested

Message to customers: **"You are a number.
We are here to process you."**

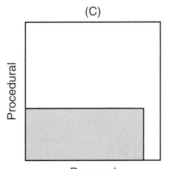

(C)

The **"Friendly Zoo"** service characteristics:

Procedural	**Personal**
Slow	Friendly
Inconsistent	Personable
Disorganized	Interested
Chaotic	Tactful

Message to customers: **"We are trying hard,
but we don't really know what we're doing."**

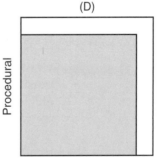

(D)

Quality Customer Service characteristics:

Procedural	**Personal**
Timely	Friendly
Efficient	Personable
Uniform	Interested
	Tactful

Message to customers: **"We care, and
we deliver."**

communicate no sense of interest in the customer and broadcast this silent message: "I don't really care about you."

The factory is skewed toward procedural efficiency (diagram B). These service providers are doing at least some things right, according to guests. They are procedurally skewed because service is timely and efficient, but the interaction is cold and impersonal. Service may be fast and efficient, but it's also unfriendly and insensitive to customers' human needs. This configuration leaves a great deal of room for improvement in the personal dimension. This type of service conveys this message to the customer: "You are a number. I am here to process you as efficiently as I can."

The friendly zoo (diagram C) is skewed toward personal warmth, the other extreme. Although service is friendly, genuine, and warm, it is also slow, inconsistent, and disorganized. Service providers may show a great deal of interest in their customers and be tactful and polite, but the inconvenience of procedural problems generally overshadows all the "warm fuzzies" otherwise provided. (It is common to see this kind of service in newly open hospitality operations that are run by inexperienced individuals.) The message to the customer from this kind of service is, "I am trying hard, but I don't really know what I am doing."

What hospitality service providers should be striving for, of course, is a service configuration as close as possible to **quality customer service,** in which both dimensions are well matched, as shown in diagram D. Even though this is labeled a full arena, the graph still reflects some possibility for improvement, because perfection is rare, if not impossible. On the whole, however, service providers cover all the important areas of the procedural and personal dimensions. With regard to procedure, service is timely, efficient, and uniform—consistently solid. The service is also personal; the service providers have a customer-friendly approach. They exude a real interest in guests as individuals. To the customer, the message is, "I care about you, and I deliver."

Chapter 4 in Review

KEY CONCEPTS

1. Quality customer service is defined as the ability to consistently meet external and internal customer needs, wants, and expectations involving procedural and personal encounters.

2. When represented in graphic form, the two dimensions of customer service, procedural and personal, can be shown to illustrate four basic patterns of meeting customer expectations: the freezer, the factory, the friendly zoo, and quality customer service.

KEY TERMS

Consistency
Customer expectations
Personal dimension
Procedural dimension
Quality customer service
The factory
The freezer
The friendly zoo

STUDY QUESTIONS/DISCUSSION STIMULATORS

1. How is the concept of consistency important to the definition of quality customer service?

2. Why do customer expectations and not organizational needs define quality customer service?

3. What are the two major dimensions of customers' customer service expectations? How would you define each dimension?

4. What happens when a customer receives a "freezer" level of service? A "factory" level of service? A "friendly zoo" level of service? A "quality" level of service?

APPLICATION INTERACTION EXERCISE 11

THE FOUR TYPES OF SERVICE AND YOU

The four types of service are graphically represented below. Under each one briefly describe a service encounter representing that type of service that you personally experienced firsthand. Tell what happened.

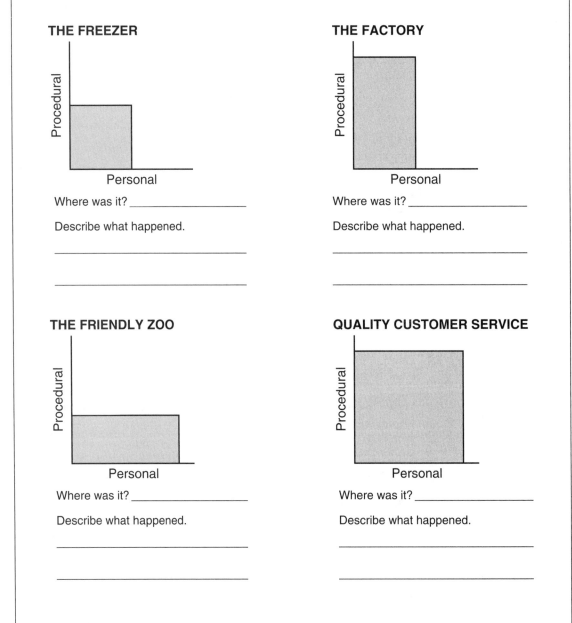

THE FREEZER

Procedural

Personal

Where was it? _____

Describe what happened.

_____

_____

THE FACTORY

Procedural

Personal

Where was it? _____

Describe what happened.

_____

_____

THE FRIENDLY ZOO

Procedural

Personal

Where was it? _____

Describe what happened.

_____

_____

QUALITY CUSTOMER SERVICE

Procedural

Personal

Where was it? _____

Describe what happened.

_____

_____

Section II

THE SYSTEM SIDE OF SERVICE—

Providing That *Procedural* Touch

5

Timing is Everything

One of the first thoughts that come to customers' minds when asked about service invariably relates to timeliness. When timeliness is mentioned, usually we think of promptness. Customers rarely have all the time in the world to wait for service. Even if we did, few of us want to wait any longer than necessary. When it comes to dining, some of us approach it from the viewpoint of "get my food so I can eat and leave." Fast-food restaurants were created to meet many of these quick-dining needs. In most full-service restaurants, promptness is usually a greater concern at breakfast and lunch than it is at dinner. But extended waits exasperate most customers whether the experience is restaurant, lodging, or travel related.

Greeting Time

Promptness is particularly important at the first step of the service encounter—the point of initial greeting. No customers enjoy standing and waiting at the greeting area of any establishment without their presence at least being acknowledged. Even if the service provider is busy with another guest or in the process of doing something else, the fact that customers have arrived needs to be noted and communicated to them. A brief "Hello, I'll be with you in a minute" or a friendly nod or smile just to let them know you are aware of them is essential. Prompt greetings at the door, at the front desk, in the dining room, in the lounge, or at any initial point of the service encounter should have top priority among hospitality service providers. If not, customers will sit and wait and wonder if anybody knows they're around.

Service Time

In addition to the timing of the initial greeting, there are three other critical timing periods for most hospitality customers: the waiting time *before* service, the waiting *during* service, and the waiting time *after* service.

FROM THE QUALITY SERVICE HALL OF SHAME

A vacationing hotel guest commented, "Since we had our four kids with us we needed extra towels in the bathroom so I called the front desk. The clerk said the towels would be right up. We waited for over ten minutes. I called again. The clerk said, 'You haven't gotten them yet?' I said, 'No.' Her response was, 'They will be right up.' We waited another ten minutes. I called again. We eventually got our towels—thirty minutes after the first call."

PRESERVICE WAITS

A major issue of preservice waits is the extent of customer choice. The question is, How much choice do customers have when deciding whether to wait? For example, when entering a restaurant that does not take reservations, customers can decide to stay or leave based on the number of people already waiting and/or the quoted wait time. In such situations, customer freedom of choice is maximized. Other hospitality situations, however, may be unable to provide such clear-cut choices. When guests arrive with reservations in hand, they tend to be precommitted to receiving service. In other words, they have already made the choice. When they are informed that, even with their reservation, they will be required to wait before they can check in, or wait before they can be seated, they are more inclined to stay because of this sense of precommitment. A second issue of preservice waits is the accuracy of the quoted wait time—the indicated length of wait time. Waits that are equal to or less than the time quoted are more acceptable than waits that extend beyond the expected time.

TIMING DURING SERVICE

Once service has begun, the next question becomes, How long does the service encounter, itself, take? Does check-in at a hotel require two, five, or ten minutes? Is the total dining experience in a restaurant fifteen minutes or two hours? How long does it take to check in at the plane terminal and to get bags checked? The answers to these timing questions vary with (1) the nature of the service operation, (2) the number of service steps involved in the total service encounter, and (3) how capacity flow is managed. Each of these affects customer expectations of appropriate timing requirements. The classic hospitality example is quick food service compared with full service. Because of the nature of the operation and number of service steps, most customers expect to spend more time receiving service at a full-service restaurant as opposed to a quick-service one. Because of varying international travel requirements and security checks, preboarding time for international flights tends to take longer than preboarding domestic and local flights. In contrast, lodging operations in all market segments have made great strides in equalizing and minimizing service times at check in. This is a direct result of their uses of capacity flow management techniques, which I discuss in more detail in the next chapter.

FROM THE QUALITY SERVICE HALL OF FAME

Many hotels and restaurants have timing standards that are incorporated into service provider training. During busy periods, a popular Tex-Mex restaurant chain stations a host right at the front door so guests are greeted immediately upon entering the restaurant. An international hotel company requires that all phones be answered within three rings. A family dining restaurant chain known for its pies has adopted a comprehensive set of service standards. Meeting customers' timing expectations is an important component of this program.

POSTSERVICE TIMING

Last, but certainly not least, is the extraordinarily critical postservice time. This includes restaurant customers waiting for their check or to receive change, hotel guests waiting to check out, and airline passengers waiting to deplane or obtain their luggage. These are the times when customers tend to be least willing to tolerate delay. Why is this? This is usually an extremely sensitive time because service has not only been completed, but more important, the customer's mind-set is already on the next set of activities on the agenda. Mentally, they have already left the respective restaurant, or hotel, or airport. Although patience may be a virtue, at this stage of the service cycle, postservice customer patience is more like a depleted natural resource. That is why postservice timing must be protected and managed very carefully.

Promptness vs. Timeliness

In this discussion of timeliness, it is important not to confuse promptness with timeliness. Promptness is always related to quickness. Timeliness is not. That is, what may be considered timely is relative to the situation and to customers' expectations. Time, after all, is relative. Customers' timing needs vary according to their moods, the circumstances, or the occasion. For example, one party in a restaurant may be in a hurry; another may want a leisurely meal and may be made to feel rushed if served as quickly as the party in a hurry. Other factors may also affect customers' timing expectations. Usually, the more expensive the service, the longer guests are willing to wait. Feeling rushed through a two-hundred-dollar meal for two, in most cases, would be a service travesty. In addition, when guest waiting time is occupied—they are engaged in a group, or are being entertained in some way—the perceived length of wait is considerably less. Moreover, many waits are made more acceptable after the service provider explains the reason for the wait and its projected duration. In contrast, un-explained waits or waits of unknown duration seem to be longer, and hence less acceptable.

Chapter 5 in Review

KEY CONCEPTS

1. Four components of timely service include greeting time, prewait time, timing during service, and postservice timing.

2. Timeliness and promptness are not necessarily the same.

3. Timeliness is relative to the service situation and the customer's expectations.

KEY TERMS

Greeting time
Postservice time
Preservice time
Promptness
Service time
Timeliness
Timing during service

STUDY QUESTIONS/DISCUSSION STIMULATORS

1. Why is timeliness a critical ingredient of quality customer service?

2. Why is greeting time particularly important?

3. What are the three components of service time? How is each defined?

4. Why is proper postservice timing particularly challenging?

5. What is the difference between promptness and timeliness?

6. Under what circumstances can service be too fast?

APPLICATION INTERACTION EXERCISE 12

YOU'VE GOT TIMING

I. Comparing Customers' Timing Expectations with Actual Waiting Times

If you are currently working in a hospitality operation, compare **guests' expectations** for the four critical waiting times below with the **average actual** waiting time.

If you are not currently working, think about a time when you went out to dinner to a restaurant. As the guest, compare your timing expectations with the actual time of service.

	Guests' Timing Expectations	Actual Waiting Time
Initial *Greeting*	_____	_____
Before Service Wait	_____	_____
During Service Wait	_____	_____
After Service Wait	_____	_____

If you have recorded a discrepancy between guests' timing expectations and the actual waiting time, what do you think can be done to provide more timely service in this hospitality operation?

_____

_____

_____

_____

_____

_____

APPLICATION INTERACTION EXERCISE 13

MANAGING TIME

A guest's acceptance (or lack of acceptance) of a wait is often based on how well the wait is being managed. With the same hospitality operation in mind that you used on the previous page, indicate below what this operation is doing to manage guest-waiting times.

1. How are guests able to occupy their waiting time?

   _____

   _____

2. How are waiting times communicated to guests?

   _____

   _____

3. How is the duration of waits explained to guests?

   _____

   _____

4. What systems are in place to help ensure waiting times are kept fair?

   _____

   _____

5. What is done to make the wait of solo guests easier?

   _____

   _____

6. Which of the above service techniques could be improved upon?

   _____

   _____

   How?

   _____

   _____

6

Getting in the Flow

Whether service is timely is often a function of how well the operation is able to maintain a smooth and even flow of service. Ideally, service should flow to the customer continuously, steadily, and incrementally. The key to any hospitality service efficiency—particularly if it is a busy place—is to maintain an *even flow* of service. The quality level of service that customers receive often depends on the service providers' ability to establish and maintain a steady flow of service.

Establishing and maintaining an incremental flow of service is more difficult than most customers imagine. Whether it is the taco stand down the street, a giant convention hotel, a theme park, or a computer-designed flight schedule, hospitality operations are made up of a complex set of systems which, in turn, are divided into numerous subsystems. Each of these parts performs a role vital to the successful operation of the whole system. Moreover, the smooth functioning of each part is dependent on the other's proper operation. The potential for a breakdown in the flow of service in any hospitality operation is therefore immense.

These various parts of the service system are in delicate balance. When the balance is maintained, customers have the best chance of receiving efficient service. When the parts are not in balance—that is, when some are overloaded—the results can be disastrous for the operation and, in turn, for the customers.

The Imbalance Ripple Effect

Here is an all too common restaurant example of the imbalance ripple effect—a time when fifty (or more) guests arrive for a banquet.

In the space of just a few minutes, the awaited guests walk through the front door. The host greets them and immediately seats them as they arrive. Because all the guests are seated at approximately the same time and most of them order before-dinner cocktails, a mass of drink orders is taken and delivered to the bartender, who is suddenly faced with nearly fifty orders. Setting up all these drinks at once takes a long time, especially if the bartender is new to the job. In the meantime, any orders placed after the rush of fifty sit and wait. Consequently, not only do the fifty banquet guests wait longer than usual for their cocktails, but also the customers who happened to arrive after the big order have to wait longer in the lounge for the bartender to catch up. This is not the end of it. The ripple effect upon the total service flow continues when the fifty dinner orders are sent to the kitchen. Because the dinner orders are all taken at the same time, the kitchen is besieged with fifty entrée orders at once. The kitchen crew utters a few expletives and gets busy, but the guests end up waiting an extended time for their dinners nevertheless. In addition, guests who are seated in the dining room after the banquet orders hit the kitchen also experience a long wait to receive their meals. And, because most of the dinners are consumed in approximately the same time, all the orders for dessert or after-dinner drinks are equally delayed.

This example illustrates how an imbalance in customer traffic can adversely affect the flow of service. Variations of this theme are played out on a daily basis in restaurants, hotels, theme parks, and travel carrier operations everywhere. A sudden rush of guests is only one example of how a breakdown can occur. Inadequate employee scheduling, equipment malfunction, food and beverage or supply shortages, new, slow, or poorly trained service providers, as well as many other unforeseen developments can cause a breakdown in a hospitality operation's service flow.

With all these sources of potential problems, it is particularly challenging to establish and maintain a proper flow of service in a busy hospitality operation. But without a smooth, incremental flow, it is virtually impossible to maintain service quality. The complexity and interdependence of the parts of a hospitality operation means that it can easily "lose its balance" by becoming overextended at one service point, thereby leading to untimely and inefficient service.

FROM THE QUALITY SERVICE HALL OF SHAME

 When a hostess in one particular busy Florida restaurant was upset at a particular server or didn't like a server, for one reason or another, she would deliberately fill that server's section with customers all at once. This not only made the server's job of greeting and serving everyone at one time more difficult, it also meant that customers were forced to wait longer than usual because of the imbalanced service flow.

Maintaining an Incremental Flow

The flow can be controlled. Procedural quality can be maintained if the operation utilizes certain techniques for creating and maintaining an incremental flow of service to customers. The operational task is to be able to break service steps into small, deliverable, incremental parts so no one part of the system becomes stressed beyond capacity at any one point. Here are ten common examples:

1. A dining reservation system that allows for incremental seating of guests

2. Premenu or limited menu selection for large dining parties

3. Food servers controlling the sequence of service within sections

4. A queuing system that allows service to take place in sequential steps

5. Lodging registration information obtained at the time of making a reservation

6. Preroom assignments for tour groups

7. Assigning plane seats at time of ticketing

8. Physical properties that make entrance and exit easy for large groups of people (no bottlenecks)

9. Plane boarding the rear seats first, on up to the front

10. Room check out by using the television in the room

Each of these is a deliberate way to process or otherwise move a large group of guests through the service system by breaking service, itself, down into manageable or otherwise palatable parts. The service provider's ability to do this well greatly impacts the customers' service experience in a positive way.

FROM THE QUALITY SERVICE HALL OF FAME

Many restaurants now provide small vibrating pagers for waiting guests. This not only allows guests to walk, shop, or hang out in the lounge without worrying about missing their call for seating but also helps reduce crowded waiting areas.

A landmark hotel on Coronado Island in Southern California offers four checkout options that make checking out quick and easy for guests. They can check out using their television in their room; they can check out over the phone by dialing a checkout extension number; they can leave a signed express checkout form at the bell desk or front desk; or they can always check out the old-fashioned way at the front desk.

Server Control of the Flow

In most full-service restaurants, servers are responsible for a certain number of tables—commonly referred to as a section. To a great degree, food servers can control the flow of service within their sections. To explain how this is done, I'll use an example of a typical section with four tables. The goal is to create a *balance* within your section. This is accomplished when each table within a section is at a different point in the sequence of service. One table is just sitting down, requiring a greeting. Another table is in the middle of the salad course. A third table is at the entrée course, and the fourth table is finishing dessert or getting ready to leave. Under these circumstances service logjams are minimized because the section is in balance.

How a host or hostess seats a section can greatly facilitate or inhibit the balance of service within a section. However, even when an entire section is seated at once, skilled food servers can adjust the timing at each individual table to get their sections into more of a balanced situation. These service heroes note which table or tables might be in more of a hurry—where promptness is a factor. They quickly get these tables started. Then they assess which table or tables may be interested in a more leisurely dining pace. (The ordering of wine or appetizers or a group deeply engrossed in conversation often indicates this.) By controlling the serving time at each table, service providers can do a great deal to bring an imbalance situation back into balance. They create this balance by having each table within their sections at varying stages of the total dining process. This, in turn, greatly facilitates a smoother flow of service to the guests.

Chapter 6 in Review

KEY CONCEPTS

1. Maintaining an even flow of service is the key to providing efficient and timely service.

2. A breakdown or imbalance in one part of the service system can adversely affect the entire service system.

3. Service flow can be maintained by breaking service down into incremental parts.

4. By being sensitive to varying customer-timing needs, service providers can control, to some degree, the balance of service within their service areas.

KEY TERMS

Balance
Imbalance ripple effect
Incremental flow

STUDY QUESTIONS/DISCUSSION STIMULATORS

1. How does the flow of service affect service timing?

2. How does the dependency of one service subsystem on another affect the flow of service within the total system?

3. How does breaking service down into incremental parts help maintain a more even flow of service?

4. What are some ways service providers can help generate a more even flow of service?

5. What are airlines and hotels currently doing to reduce service bottlenecks?

APPLICATION INTERACTION EXERCISE 14

MAINTAINING THAT FLOW

If you are currently working as a service provider, respond to the questions below according to how your hospitality operation is managing the flow of service in order to meet customer expectations?

OR

If you are not currently working, think about a time when you were a guest at a hotel or restaurant. How did that hospitality operation and service provider(s) manage the flow of the service you received?

1. How is the physical layout of the service area designed to facilitate a flow of service?

_____

_____

_____

2. How does the scheduling of service providers facilitate a flow of service?

_____

_____

_____

3. How are advance reservations or prebookings used to manage the flow?

_____

_____

_____

4. What adjustments are made for large groups so a flow of service is maintained?

_____

_____

_____

(continued)

5. What queuing system (line formation) is used to assist the flow of service?

_____

_____

_____

6. How can service providers, themselves, control the flow of service during the various steps of service provided?

_____

_____

_____

7. What systems are in place that expedite the completion of service such as early or express checkouts?

_____

_____

_____

8. If the service unit experiences a logjam, what other units in the operation are effected by this?

_____

_____

_____

9. What is the most common situation that contributes to a breakdown in the flow of service?

_____

_____

_____

10. What do you think can be done to reduce or eliminate this breakdown in the flow?

_____

_____

_____

7

AN-TIC-I-PA-TION

Another component of quality service expected by hospitality consumers is effective anticipation. Imbalances in the flow of service can and should be anticipated by customer-attuned service providers. Problems and delays in service need to be foreseen and adjustments made. Adequate staffing is a key ingredient in such a situation. Another is having a flexible service team available so individuals can be easily reassigned to service areas requiring customer attention.

One Step Ahead

Effective anticipation means that hospitality service providers constantly remain one step ahead of customers' needs. Knowing ahead of time the approximate number of customers that will be requiring service most certainly makes effective anticipation easier. This requires a reliable and easy-to-use database. This information can provide accurate projections not only for near- and long-term future customer counts and sales but also can provide accurate historical data so service impact can be anticipated as to the season, the month, day of the week, and time of day.

FROM THE QUALITY SERVICE HALL OF SHAME

One dining customer commented, "I took the kids out to dinner the other night to a busy, fun-oriented family restaurant. The food was good, but I had to ask for the most basic items that should have come automatically. I had to ask the server twice for drink refills (which were free). I had to ask for a booster chair, when they could clearly see I had a small child with me. I even had to ask for extra napkins to help get the kids cleaned up after the meal. What ever happened to good service anyway? How frustrating. At least the kids had a good time."

A Sensitive Service Area

Nothing upsets a guest more than arriving at a hotel with a confirmed reservation in hand and being told there are no rooms available. How and why does this happen? Most large hotels use a computerized system to help them anticipate and manage room occupancy. It is referred to as yield management. Yield management is a system of anticipating what the occupancy of the hotel will be for a given night. It is cost-effective for a lodging establishment to maximize the number of rooms sold each night. A yield management system tells the hotel how many rooms to book based on no-show rates, current stays and anticipated checkouts, reservations, and other factors. If the system works, guest needs and wants for lodging are met, and everybody is happy. If it fails, the guests are left holding nothing but their bags while the hotel enjoys the revenue from its 100 percent occupancy.

Anticipation Cues

At the service encounter level, hospitality service providers are anticipating effectively when they provide service *before* the guest asks for it. This requires not only knowing *what* the guest will need but also *when*. To be able to do this requires that service providers look for certain cues, or indicators, to help anticipate possible customer needs. Here are a few restaurant examples.

- A high chair and extra napkins already at the table when a family with small children sits down

- Extra napkins to go with finger food

- Two forks with a single dessert order

- A spoon to replace one dropped by the guest

- "Doggie bags" when food is left on a plate

- Coffee refills when cups are low

Each of these is provided without customers having to ask for them.

FROM THE QUALITY SERVICE HALL OF FAME

Another dining customer commented, "I couldn't believe this small seafood restaurant my husband and I went to in San Francisco. I turned my head to look for the waiter, and he was at our side immediately as if he had anticipated my request. Our water and wineglasses were never empty. He brought extra forks with each course, extra lemon wedges, and a second helping of bread without a word from us. That guy was on top of it. What a pleasure."

On the lodging side, we see effective anticipation in the following ways:

- When an alert front desk assistant calls housekeeping for a delivery of extra towels to a room where a large family has just checked in

- When the front desk service provider makes sure he or she is well stocked with a variety of personal toiletry items that guests often forget to pack from home

Fight attendants anticipate when they have plenty of pillows, blankets, and personal toiletry items available on long flights, in addition to infant toiletries for small passengers who just might need them.

Skillful anticipation comes from being sensitive to such indicators as group size, customer age, how customers are dressed, what customers have said, as well as their body language and tone of voice. Each of these possible indicators becomes an anticipation cue. Reading them carefully and accurately allows service providers to remain one step ahead of their customers.

Chapter 7 in Review

KEY CONCEPTS

1. Effective anticipation requires being one step ahead of customer needs.

2. Accurately anticipating room occupancy is a particularly sensitive service area in the lodging industry.

3. Service providers can better anticipate customer needs by learning to identify certain anticipatory cues.

KEY TERMS

Anticipation cues
One step ahead
Yield management

STUDY QUESTIONS/DISCUSSION STIMULATORS

1. How do reliable databases facilitate effective anticipation of service needs?

2. Why is hotel yield management a sensitive service area?

3. How do we know when service providers are anticipating effectively?

4. From your experience, what are some common customer cues that serve as anticipation markers for hospitality service providers?

APPLICATION INTERACTION EXERCISE 15

ONE STEP AHEAD

Fifteen common customer types and hospitality encounter situations are listed below. **What might a customer need or want in each situation? What service could you provide *before* a customer asks for it?** Indicate your responses in the spaces provided.

1. Large groups _____

2. Children _____

3. Teens _____

4. Young Adults _____

5. Middle-aged Couple _____

6. Business Traveler _____

7. Seniors _____

8. Handicapped guests _____

9. Guest orders a messy food item_____

10. Guest has trouble understanding English _____

11. Guest indicates she is in a hurry _____

12. Guest is dressed in formal attire_____

13. The Rush Period_____

14. Guest leaves food on plate_____

15. Empty beverage glasses _____

16. Other indicators, specific to your operation or experience

_____

_____

8

Communicate, Communicate, Communicate

■ ■ ■ ■ ■ ■ ■ ■ ■ ■ ■   ■   ■

Hospitality service providers will have a difficult time anticipating guests' needs unless communication flows well within and between the various parts of the operation. Effective communication occurs only when messages are timely, precise in meaning, and thorough in content. Unfortunately, in the realities of the everyday hospitality world, achieving this is extraordinarily difficult. Communication breakdown tends to be the rule rather than the exception.

Communication Breakdown

A breakdown in communication leads to misunderstandings; misunderstandings lead to mistakes; and the consequence of mistakes is usually poor customer service. Yet hospitality customers need and expect successful communication as part and parcel of the complete service encounter. Successful communication leads to understanding; understanding helps systems and procedures run as they should; and properly functioning systems help contribute to high-quality customer service.

The rub for hospitality service providers in all of this is that the odds are stacked against successful communication. Within the complete communication loop, it only takes *one* source of breakdown for the entire process to fail. A complete communication exchange includes (1) the sender, (2) the message, (3) the receiver, and (4) feedback. Effective communication requires success at each of these four critical junctures. A breakdown can potentially occur at any one of these points for a variety of reasons.

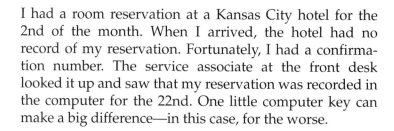

FROM THE QUALITY SERVICE HALL OF SHAME

I had a room reservation at a Kansas City hotel for the 2nd of the month. When I arrived, the hotel had no record of my reservation. Fortunately, I had a confirmation number. The service associate at the front desk looked it up and saw that my reservation was recorded in the computer for the 22nd. One little computer key can make a big difference—in this case, for the worse.

A frustrated lunch customer wrote, "I ordered a grilled chicken sandwich. I was served a chicken salad. I said to the server, 'I ordered a grilled chicken sandwich.' Her response was 'You said chicken salad. That is what I wrote down.' I responded, 'I said chicken sandwich.' Then she said, 'Are you sure you don't want the chicken salad?' I was so frustrated (and hungry) I just kept the salad. I felt better after I had eaten and left a penny for her tip."

SENDER BREAKDOWN

Communication can break down right at the source—with the sender. Whether the senders are customers, managers, or service providers, the consequence is the same: a garbled message. Here are a few possibilities: The sender may—

1. Use poor timing (e.g., while the receiver is busy doing something else).

2. Choose the wrong method of communicating (e.g., written instead of spoken).

3. Choose the wrong place (e.g., in public rather than in private).

4. Use an inappropriate tone of voice (alienating receivers).

5. Use a poor choice of words or use the wrong words.

6. Use behavioral signals that differ from the verbal message.

MESSAGE BREAKDOWN

The message itself or the transmission of the message may go afoul. Here are a few examples. The message may be—

1. Too long.

2. Too short, leaving out information crucial to the receiver's understanding.

3. Too general or ambiguous.

4. Communicated too quickly, resulting in incomplete reception

5. Erroneous or incorrect.

6. Not transmitted (e.g., the computer crashes, or it gets lost in a pile of papers).

RECEIVER BREAKDOWN

The sender may do everything right and the message itself may be fine, but if it is not received, no communication takes place. Here are six examples of a breakdown on the receiving end. The receiver may—

1. Be busy, preoccupied, or otherwise distracted.

2. Fail to understand the words in the message.

3. Have an emotional block toward the sender (e.g., fear, anger, and dislike).

4. Believe he already knows what the message will be and thus fails to pay proper attention to it.

5. Be tired.

6. Be confused.

FEEDBACK BREAKDOWN

Communication in which messages are sent with no opportunity for the sender to find out whether the message was received (commonly called *one-way* communication) leads to communication breakdown and misunderstanding. The major culprits perpetuating one-way communication in hospitality operations are the following:

1. Sender simply assumes the message has been received as intended.

2. Sender fails to seek, demand, or otherwise encourage message feedback.

3. Receiver fails to provide feedback to the sender, whether it is sought or not.

FROM THE QUALITY SERVICE HALL OF FAME

This quote is from a satisfied quick food service customer. "The order taking system at your restaurants is great. Your drive-thru speakers really work. I can hear the person taking my order very clearly without any static. And the order taker always repeats my order to make sure it is correct. I like that part. Then I know they have it right. Then the order taker tells me what the exact price will be at the window so I can be ready. And the entire service crew always seems to be in such a good mood. It's amazing these days to still receive such great service, but I always seem to get it at your restaurants."

Effective Hospitality Communication

With the odds stacked against it, quality customer service requires that communication systems not only work, but also work well. This happens when *the message is received exactly as it was intended.* Until then, the potential for a breakdown exists. Without feedback, senders never know whether they have communicated. This is why communication requires continuous "care and feeding" on the part of hospitality organizations.

Quality service expectations from guests require that communication is successful between the customer and the service provider and also within the operation. A complete treatise on effective communication techniques is beyond the scope of this book. In its place, I offer twenty examples of what customers expect from communication exchanges with hospitality service providers *and* communication among the entire service delivery team.

1. The service provider to have a record of their reservation after they've made one

2. To receive the exact meal that they ordered and prepared as requested

3. The accommodations that they have requested and have been told they would receive

4. An understanding and empathetic ear when there is a problem

5. To be able to talk to a manager when they request it

6. The person providing service to speak clearly and intelligibly

7. The front desk representative to look at them when talking rather than at the computer screen

8. Food servers to repeat food and beverage orders

9. Front desk service representative to repeat the service requested from them

10. A system that provides feedback if they choose to use it

11. Service providers who are willing to listen to what they have to say

12. Their messages expeditiously communicated within and through the organization as needed to the appropriate person or persons

13. Sincere gratitude communicated to them for their patronage

14. Quick service, if they indicate they are in a hurry

15. Their food delivered to the table without the server asking, "Who ordered the roast beef?"

16. The wait for service to be the time (or before) that they were quoted

17. Their food server to ask how their meal is *after* they have taken a bite or two

18. Short and clear oral explanations of the daily specials with prices attached

19. Food servers to ask, "How is your [item ordered]," and to mean it

20. Their name used and pronounced correctly

Chapter 8 in Review

KEY CONCEPTS

1. Effective communication occurs when the message received is exactly as it was intended.

2. Communication breakdown is easy; effective communication is difficult.

3. A complete communication exchange includes the sender, the message, the receiver, and feedback.

4. Customers expect effective communication between themselves and their service providers and between the entire service team.

KEY TERMS

Effective communication
Feedback
Message
Receiver
Sender

STUDY QUESTIONS/DISCUSSION STIMULATORS

1. Why does communication breakdown tend to be the rule rather than the exception in hospitality organizations?

2. Within a complete communication exchange, why are the odds stacked against effective communication?

3. In a hospitality service environment, how can communication breakdown be minimized?

APPLICATION INTERACTION EXERCISE **16**

SERVICE PROVIDER COMMUNICATION

Note: You may respond to this exercise as a service provider or as a customer.

I. What methods of communication are used most often in this hospitality operation?

Oral?   Written?   Electronic?   Body Language?

1. With guests _____

2. With service providers _____

3. With other units in the operation _____

II. What are the most common sources of breakdown? Check your responses. And then indicate what might possibly help eliminate this breakdown in communication.

Write Possible Solution Here

A. From the Sender

   1. _____ timing

   2. _____ method

   3. _____ place

   4. _____ tone

   5. _____ choice of words

   6. _____ conflicting behavior signals

B. From the Message

   1. _____ too long

   2. _____ too short

   3. _____ too general

   4. _____ too quick

   5. _____ wrong message

   6. _____ not transmitted

C. From the Receiver

   1. _____ busy

   2. _____ lack of understanding

   3. _____ emotional block

   4. _____ prejudges message

(continued)

Write Possible Solution Here

5. _____ tired

6. _____ confused

D. From the Feedback

1. _____ no feedback sought

2. _____ no feedback offered

E. Add your own: _____

III. What are the customers' communication needs and wants?

Note: Customer needs and wants often reflect two different criterion for quality service. You can respond below as a service provider or as a customer.

Customer Needs: Needs are service imperatives. It is necessary to satisfy a service need for the service encounter to be considered successful.

Customer Wants: Wants are important to the customer but, although desirable to satisfy, may not be imperative or absolutely necessary for the service encounter to be considered successful. However, providing for customer wants increases an operation's competitive advantage.

A. *As a service provider, my customers need the following communication skills from me.*

OR

As a customer, I need the following communication skills from my service provider.

(Indicate your response in the space below.)

_____

_____

B. *As a service provider, my customers often want the following communication skills from me. Providing for these wants makes us more competitive.*

OR

As a customer, I want my service providers to have the following communication skills.

(Indicate your response in the space below.)

_____

_____

9
Feedback—Food for Success

One way hospitality service providers can facilitate effective communication systems is to have an active and reliable system of obtaining feedback from customers. Customers not only want it, they expect it. This component of quality service is about finding out what customers think and feel about their *experiences* as consumers of the hospitality products provided by you. An effective feedback system can tell you whether customers are satisfied or dissatisfied, whether they want more or less, or whether they want something entirely different. Customer feedback tells you how you are doing according to your customers. It paves the way to serving them better.

Customer Feedback Is Indispensable

Without feedback, problems or breakdowns may go unnoticed and unresolved. Very often, customer feedback is the first step in uncovering a problem. So whether the shortcoming is slow service, salty soup, a failed request, a less than desirable room, or a rude service provider, it is imperative than customers provide feedback.

FROM THE QUALITY SERVICE HALL OF SHAME

Upon receiving completed hotel guest survey forms, one particular front desk clerk would throw them in the trash if the guests had made any negative comments.

Customer Feedback Must Be Encouraged

The problem, however, is that most customers don't like to complain. Many of them may be uncomfortable or embarrassed when asked to provide honest feedback. Others may not want to make a fuss about something that's easier to forget, ignore, or not mention. Typically, patrons will complain among themselves, but when the server asks how things are, they say, "Fine!" Others will suffer in silence and simply never return. In fact, statistics suggest that for every complaint a hospitality operation receives, the operation can assume that there are approximately twenty-six other customers who have a similar complaint but fail to register it. The challenge becomes one of making it easy and convenient for guests to provide feedback.

Specific Feedback

Many service providers (particularly food servers) use the proverbial, "How is everything?" Usually the customer's response is, "Okay," whether "everything" is or not. When requesting oral feedback, the first skill service providers need to learn is to ask a *specific* question related to the guest's experience. For example, tableside, it is better to ask a guest who has ordered and received a steak, "How is your steak? Is it cooked to order?" This is a specific question customized to the guest's experience. When a hotel guest has requested certain accommodations upon check-in, the front desk representative can call the room a few minutes after check-in to determine whether the specific request has been received and to what extent the guest is satisfied. These types of oral feedback increase the chances that meaningful feedback will be obtained.

Person-to-Person Feedback

In addition to asking specific questions of guests, other means of soliciting person-to-person feedback may be utilized. One of the more useful feedback devices in the hospitality industry is for managers and service providers to get out and talk person-to-person with guests, spending time chatting with them, and getting to know them. The entire organization should encourage this form of customer interaction for the good of the overall operation.

FROM THE QUALITY SERVICE HALL OF FAME

Many hospitality companies are making full use of the Internet to obtain customer feedback. Their Web sites are easily accessible, and feedback links are clearly indicated and user friendly. Customers can respond to a structured questionnaire as well as an open-ended comment section. Another link provides a summary of all the changes made and responses to valued customer comments.

Multiple Approaches

If customer feedback is to be truly successful, however, service providers need to move beyond relying exclusively on oral responses for obtaining customer feedback. A more structured system can be put into place. Written response forms, mailed surveys, phone surveys, and organized focus groups are examples of a more structured approach. On the low-tech end, some hospitality operations have installed suggestion boxes for customers to register their ideas and reactions to their experiences. Others have gone high tech by using Web sites in the same way. Whatever form the method of feedback takes, it remains vital, from a customer's perspective, to take an active and sincere interest in encouraging customer feedback.

It is also important for the service provider to set an open, relaxed, and receptive atmosphere for customer feedback. Feedback needs to be received in the same spirit in which it is given. Service providers must be receptive to customers' remarks. They should genuinely thank the customers for their comments. Whether a customer offers positive or negative feedback, the hospitality service provider should always receive it with sincere interest and gratitude.

Chapter 9 in Review

KEY CONCEPTS

1. Customer feedback is a crucial element to providing quality customer service.

2. Feedback should be made easy for the customer.

3. When seeking feedback orally, asking a specific question is better than asking a general one.

4. The best hospitality customer feedback systems include multiple approaches.

KEY TERMS

Customer feedback
Multiple approaches
Person-to-person feedback

STUDY QUESTIONS/DISCUSSION STIMULATORS

1. Why is customer feedback so important to providing quality customer service?

2. Why are many hospitality customers reluctant to provide negative feedback?

3. What are some ways customer feedback can be made easier?

4. Of the several multiple approaches to obtaining customer feedback mentioned in this chapter, which ones do you think are most effective? Why?

APPLICATION INTERACTION EXERCISE 17

CUSTOMER FEEDBACK

I. As a service provider working in a hospitality operation OR as a customer of a hospitality operation, describe how feedback is obtained.

A. *How* is the feedback obtained?

_____

_____

B. *Who* obtains it?

_____

_____

C. *When* is it obtained?

_____

_____

D. *Where* is it obtained?

_____

_____

II. If you are working or have worked as a service provider, how is customer feedback used in the operation to improve service?

A. Who sees the feedback? With whom is it shared?

_____

_____

B. What are the consequences? What happens? What are the rewards?

_____

_____

III. Based on your experience as a customer or service provider, how can hospitality customer feedback be improved?

_____

_____

10

To Be or Not To Be Accommodating?

Proper accommodation requires proper anticipation as well as communication. Customers want and need accommodating service systems. This means that service systems need to be designed so service can be flexible and adaptable to widely diverse customer needs. In particular, accommodation means not requiring customers to adapt to rigid policies and procedures of the hospitality operation. The key to customer accommodation is being able to respond in a positive way to a special request, one that is out of the ordinary, beyond the "normal." Examples of accommodating service in a food service environment include—

- Being able and willing to provide separate checks upon request to large parties

- Accepting menu substitutions, additions to, or subtractions from menu items

- Being willing and able to make changes in orders after they have been placed

- Being willing and able to put all service under one roof on one bill

- Going out of your way to grant reasonable, but unusual guest requests.

FROM THE QUALITY SERVICE HALL OF SHAME

A fine-dining guest commented, "My wife and I had just finished an exquisite meal. I asked if we could have one dessert split. The waiter replied that the chef never allowed the splitting of desserts because doing so ruins the presentation. So I asked if we could at least have one dessert served with two forks. That request was okay. It evidently fell within the rules of the house."

A late sleeper related this incident. "It was noon on a Saturday. I had just gotten up and was in the mood for ham and eggs. I went down to the hotel's dining room to have some breakfast. The server informed me that they quit serving breakfast at 11:30. All she could say was, 'I'm sorry.' So I asked for a ham sandwich with a side of scrambled eggs. She said that they didn't serve eggs of any kind after 11:30, much less on the side. So I ended up with a ham on rye. All I could think of was Jack Nicholson in that famous scene from the movie *Five Easy Pieces*. I wish I had his nerve."

In the lodging sector, special requests may be made for—

- Certain rooms with specific features

- Certain amenities beyond the usual

- Unusual checkout times

- Requests to keep certain animals in a room

- Storage of special items

- Requests for extending the number of people in one room

FROM THE QUALITY SERVICE HALL OF FAME

 A few years ago, a major hotel in Anaheim, California had all service providers wear a badge on their uniform that said, "The Answer is 'Yes.' Now, What's the Question?" If that's not trying to be accommodating, I don't know what is.

Hard to Say "Yes"—Easy to Say "No"

Being willing or able to accommodate special or unusual requests from customers presents a challenge to hospitality service providers. The reason for this is these special requests usually require that service providers do something that they don't usually do—something out of the ordinary or normal routine. This means that in order to satisfy such requests service providers have to do something extraordinary—that is, work harder or longer, or at a minimum be inconvenienced. This is why it is easier for many hospitality service providers to say "No." They don't want to be inconvenienced, otherwise bothered, or certainly work any harder or longer than they have to. In contrast, quality service providers will try to say "Yes" to special and unusual requests even though they know by doing so that they are accepting a greater job burden. By being accommodating these service winners are accepting the responsibility and summons of meeting special requests. Being an accommodating hospitality service provider is indeed a quality service challenge.

The reality is no hospitality operation or service provider is able to say "Yes" to all requests. Some are impossible. Some may be illegal. Additionally, every hospitality operation is bound by a set of health and safety requirements. Yet, the more you and your operation can respond in the affirmative to unusual or special requests, the more your accommodation quotient goes up, which, in turn, increases the quality level of the service that you are providing.

(Note that in this chapter the term accommodation refers to flexible service systems. The use of this term in this context should not be confused with the use of the term in the lodging industry to refer to physical factors such as room accommodations.)

Chapter 10 in Review

KEY CONCEPTS

1. Hospitality customers expect accommodating service systems.

2. Accommodating special and unusual requests from customers requires flexible and adaptable service systems and service providers.

3. Being accommodating presents a special quality service challenge.

KEY TERM

Accommodation

STUDY QUESTIONS/DISCUSSION STIMULATORS

1. As a hospitality customer, have you ever made a special request of a service provider? How was it received?

2. As a hospitality service provider, what unusual requests have you received? How have you responded? Why?

3. When it comes to granting special or unusual requests from a hospitality customer, why is it hard to say "Yes" and easy to say "No"?

APPLICATION INTERACTION EXERCISE **18**

ACCOMMODATION

I. Responding as a service provider or a hospitality customer, rate how accommodating a specific hospitality operation is from your experience.

Name of operation: _____

Check the service that this operation provides without any questions when guests request them. Then cite a specific example of the situations you checked.

1. _____ Substituting one product for another

   Example:

2. _____ Providing for separate billings and/or checks

   Example:

3. _____ Granting special product requests

   Example:

4. _____ Supplying special product needs

   Example:

5. _____ Utilizing special or unique processes or procedures

   Example:

6. _____ Providing special timing requirements

   Example:

(continued)

7. _____ Allowing special payment requests

Example:

8. _____ Providing special transportation requests

Example:

9. _____ Other

Example:

II. What are some customer requests that are impossible for this operation to accommodate? Why can't these requests be granted?

_____

_____

_____

_____

_____

_____

III. What could this hospitality operation possibly do to become more accommodating?

_____

_____

_____

_____

_____

_____

Section III

THE HUMAN SIDE
OF SERVICE—

Providing That *Personal* Touch

11

The Four Basic Customer Service Needs

The remaining chapters in this book focus on the human side of service—what customers want personally. In contrast to the procedural dimension of quality service, this dimension includes not only human thoughts, but also attitudes, emotions, and feelings as well—in other words, your humanness and the humanness of your customers. It is from this essential humanness that the four basic customer needs emerge. To one degree or another, all hospitality customers have them. That is why understanding and appreciating the four basic customer service needs is vital to understanding and appreciating where hospitality customers are coming from. Moreover, this is where the roots of quality service are founded—in the customer. In sum, these four needs serve as the foundation for all the remaining customer expectations discussed in this book. The four basic customer service needs are—

1. The need to be understood

2. The need to feel welcome

3. The need for comfort

4. The need to feel important

Because they are so important, we need to take a closer look at each one.

The Need to Be Understood

This particular customer need goes beyond the communication system expectations I addressed in the procedural dimension of quality service. Although the need to promote effective communication on a procedural level remains, there is also the need of customers to be understood on a deeper, emotional level. Meeting this need requires particular attention on the part of hospitality service providers. Not only do you have to send and receive clear messages, meeting this guest need requires you to "tune-in" to your guests. This requires a particular sensitivity—the ability to establish *rapport* with guests. This means connecting with customers on a feeling level—getting to enjoy them and having them enjoy you in return. Meeting this need also means being able to see the service encounter through the eyes of the guest. This is known as *empathy*. The ability to empathize reflects understanding your customer on an emotional level. To make understanding the customer even more complicated, the words customers use to communicate often fail to convey the real message of what they are trying to say. Skillful service providers must interpret—search for the "real" meaning in order to fully understand guests. When you are able to do all this, you are on your way.

The Need to Feel Welcome

Hospitality customers need to feel like they belong, that they are insiders, that you, their service provider, is happy to see them and that their business is important to you. Through the attitudes that you convey and the words you use, you are capable of making your customers feel welcome or unwelcome. Many guests come to hospitality situations for the first time. They may be somewhat intimidated—unsure of themselves—not sure they are dressed appropriately or how to act. In addition, their own array of personal insecurities may compound the situation even further. Under these circumstances, your job is to set your guests at ease. Make sure your tone of voice is reassuring. Help them when necessary. Answer questions. Be patient. Explain things thoroughly. Let them know what is happening and what will be happening. No guest should ever be made to feel awkward or ill at ease. Let them know you are glad to see them. In short, make them feel welcome.

The Need for Comfort

Whether dining, lodging, clubs, theme parks, or travel, the hospitality industry is about comfort. But comfort is traditionally thought about in physical terms—comfortable seats, rooms, beds, lighting, ambience, and so forth. These represent important hospitality tangibles. But this book is focusing on hospitality intangibles. So how does this need for comfort fit in?

The need for comfort I am discussing here deals with *psychological* comfort. This incorporates customers' needs of assurance that they will be taken care of properly and their feelings of confidence that you will meet their needs. This need is an extension of the need to feel welcome. It goes beyond the need to belong to the need to be totally taken care of. It is concerned with customer needs for hassle-free service—service with no glitches, no worries, no stress, no anxieties. Therefore, it is your job as a hospitality service provider to create such an environment for all your customers. This means generating a psychological atmosphere of relaxation and enjoyment, which, after all, is what hospitality is all about.

The Need to Feel Important

Of the four basic customer service needs, this is the one as a hospitality service provider that you will probably most readily see. Why? Because all hospitality guests are important and have a need to feel that way. This need reflects the fundamental human ego needs that we all have. All of us want to feel special, important, and that we matter. That is why no hospitality guest should ever be made to feel demeaned, belittled, or embarrassed—under any circumstances. And, like us, some hospitality customers have stronger ego needs than others. Some customers may require more special attention (often referred to as ego "stroking"). This level of service should not be viewed as something extra but rather as a natural extension of a hospitality service provider's job. Another reality of the hospitality business is as the price tag for hospitality services increases, the need to feel important becomes more evident in guests. When guests are paying top dollar for whatever services they are receiving, they want and expect (consciously or unconsciously) their ability to pay for it recognized and respected. In many cases, they want to be treated with deference. They feel that they have earned it. Providing quality service demands that these needs be respected. But fulfilling this need cannot and should not be limited to the rich and famous. Regardless of economic level or social status, all guests, no matter what amount of money is involved, need to be put on a pedestal. At the moment of each and every service encounter—the moment of truth—*all* customers remain our reason for being. Each and every one is inherently important. This understanding lies at the very heart of the customer service perspective.

Chapter 11 in Review

KEY CONCEPTS

1. The four basic customer service needs play an integral role in satisfying all personal customer service expectations.

2. Meeting guest needs for understanding, to feel welcome, for comfort, and to feel important embody the customer service perspective.

KEY TERMS

Customer service perspective
Ego
Empathy
Psychological comfort
Rapport
Tuning-in

STUDY QUESTIONS/DISCUSSION STIMULATORS

1. What is so special about the four basic customer service needs? What role do they play in providing quality customer service?

2. How does the need to be understood go beyond procedural customer communication expectations?

3. How does the need to feel welcome relate to customer insecurities or intimidation?

4. What is meant by the term "psychological comfort"? How can this customer need be met?

5. Why does the customer need to feel important tend to become more evident as the price of hospitality increases?

6. How does meeting all four basic customer needs relate to the customer service perspective?

APPLICATION INTERACTION EXERCISE 19

THE FOUR BASIC CUSTOMER SERVICE NEEDS

As a hospitality service provider, what can you do to address each of the four basic customer service needs?

To help my customers feel *understood*, I can—

_____

_____

_____

_____

To help my customers feel *welcome*, I can—

_____

_____

_____

_____

To help my customers feel *comfortable*, I can—

_____

_____

_____

_____

To help my customers feel *important*, I can—

_____

_____

_____

_____

12

It's All About Attitude

Performing any job involves human relations. Some jobs require more interactions than others, but few jobs depend more on effective human-relation skills than being a hospitality service provider. Because the attitudes we exhibit largely determine the degree of success we experience in human relations (on as well as off the job), the attitude you exhibit toward customers contributes directly to the quality of service rendered. Our attitudes often "shout" so loudly that others are unable to hear our words, particularly in a service encounter. As a service provider, every move you make and every word you speak is colored by your attitude.

The attitudes exhibited by hospitality service providers are important indicators of your personal human-relation skills, as well as the extent to which you are meeting the four basic customer service needs. The problem with attitudes, however, is that they are elusive. Attitudes are states of mind, internal feelings and thoughts that subtly translate themselves into behavior and speech. In other words, they can be known only through their external manifestations—behavior and conversation. Because attitudes are communicated in these ways, customers use them as important cues in evaluating the quality of service they receive.

Attitude: Body Language

One way attitudes are communicated to guests is through body language. In fact, communication experts maintain that our body language, the silent way our actions and posture show our thoughts and feelings, conveys from 50 to 70 percent of the total message in a typical two-person conversation. Much of the meaning of what we communicate is actually colored by such nonverbal mannerisms as eye movement, hand gestures, and posture. Because body language shows so much of what a person is communicating, we can use our knowledge of it to interpret the messages service providers are broadcasting to customers.

Facial expressions are worth a thousand words. They tell customers whether you are relaxed and under control or hurried and rushed. Facial expressions have been called a person's "ambassador" to the world. They silently communicate moods, attitudes, and emotional states. When you like your job, it shows. In contrast, tense lips, a wrinkled forehead, and an icy stare tell customers that things are probably not going well. These negative expressions can eventually tarnish the customers' experience.

A smile on your face is a wonderful thing to see. It is not uncommon, however, for service providers to get so busy performing the mechanical aspects of their jobs that they forget about the importance of a smile. Smiles can easily get lost in the shuffle of getting things done. Nevertheless, nothing creates rapport like a pleasant, natural, comfortable smile.

Eye contact is another important body language cue you make. Making eye contact with customers communicates sincerity, interest, and trustworthiness. In contrast, lack of eye contact reflects disinterest and insincerity. Nothing is so irritating to many guests as having a service provider approach them and then proceed to look at everything else in the room except them.

Eye contact is vital in all interactions with customers, but it is particularly important when a problem or complaint arises. The best way for service providers to communicate that they really don't care about a customer's concern is to avoid eye contact. It's a way of ignoring customers, or, at best, keeping them at a safe distance. It's a great defense mechanism, but it certainly is a poor way to deal with customer complaints. On the other hand, when you can look a customer right in the eye, apologize, and promise to make things right, the customer should at least feel better about the situation.

Hand and body movement is another form of silent communication. When you cross your arms over your chest, you may be communicating an unwillingness to communicate or a desire to defend yourself in some way. Flailing arms can reflect awkwardness, discomfort, or nervousness. Pointed fingers, jabs, and clenched fists also send negative signals. None of these gestures particularly contribute to a customer's positive service experience.

Slouched posture or shuffling feet give the impression that you lack confidence and self-discipline or that you are just plain tired. In contrast, a deliberate, spirited walk with erect, natural body movements and posture generates confidence and enthusiasm.

Proper grooming is another way you show your attitude of concern for customers. Clean faces, hands, fingernails, and clothes remain the bottom line of acceptable hospitality. Anything less is totally unacceptable. A subtler but equally important point is that you should avoid placing pencils in your hair or in any way touching your face, nose, or hair. Any behavior of this kind can communicate an uncaring attitude on your part, and a lack of concern in following basic health and cleanliness standards.

Personal and friendly body language can make the difference between a mundane hospitality experience and an exceptional one. We need to appreciate and understand what we are broadcasting to our customers by our nonverbal behavior. When body language communicates attitudes of welcoming, openness, a willingness to listen, and a concern for customers' welfare, we are making an effort to provide a quality service experience for customers. The clincher comes when these positive forms of silent communication are supported and reinforced by positive verbal communication.

FROM THE QUALITY SERVICE HALL OF SHAME

A hospitality student at a local college was hired as a summer intern at a private beach club in charge of dispensing towels, sand chairs, and umbrellas. After one week on the job, the club general manager began hearing complaints about her from members and fellow service providers alike. It seems that if she had anything to say it tended to be negative. Something was always wrong. The sun was too hot, the wind too gusty, the beach too crowded. You name it, and she would have something negative to say about it. It came as no surprise to anyone at the club that this intern was asked to leave before the end of the season.

A ttitude: Tone of Voice

Words may convey 50 percent or less of any given message, but they are still an important factor in service quality. We can interpret verbal skills in two ways: what is said and how it is said. Sometimes *the way* in which certain words are spoken takes on more significance and meaning than the words themselves. Attitudes are exhibited through the intonations of the words spoken and the emphasis placed on certain selected words. Identical words can communicate a variety of different meanings depending on vocal intonation. For example, with different intonations, the words, *"good evening"* can reflect any of the following meanings:

- I'm really glad to see you.

- I recognize you. Glad to see you again.

- What are you doing here?

- I'm too busy. Don't bother me now.

- I'm bored and couldn't care less about you.

- Good-bye. Come again.

Tone of voice also includes the emphasis placed on a particular word within a sentence. The selected emphatic word in the sentence can alter the entire message communicated. For example, the question, "May I bring you anything else?" can convey at least four different messages, depending on what word in the question is emphasized.

Emphasis	Meaning Communicated
May *I* bring you anything else?	I want to deliver it myself.
May I bring *you* anything else?	I want to serve you personally.
May I bring you *anything* else?	I'll bring you what ever you want.
May I bring you anything *else*?	There's really nothing you should need.

The appropriate tone of voice for a hospitality service encounter may vary with the setting, circumstances, and nature of the service rendered. Some environments may require an informal tone, whereas others may demand a more formal approach. In general, however, we can say that hospitality consumers want a pleasant tone of voice, and one that is not monotone, but has a variation in pitch, or tone inflection. Customers also prefer energy and enthusiasm reflected in voice tones, but not at a rate so fast you cannot be understood. My overall general advice for hospitality service providers would be to *put a smile into your voice*. Usually, the best tone of voice is a friendly tone of voice, one that reflects warmth as well as concern. Each of these communicates a positive attitude toward the customer.

Attitude Metamorphosis

A common hospitality phenomenon, but rarely recognized and little understood, is what I call attitude metamorphosis. During the course of a service day, it is natural for attitudes of service providers to gradually, or sometimes suddenly, decline. Positive attitudes are never permanent, but sometimes they are longer lasting than at other times. What contributes to this negative shift in attitude exhibited by hospitality service providers? The answer is, quality customer service requires *feeling* on the part of the service provider. And when feelings are needed to perform a job, a great deal of energy is spent. This spent energy is known as *emotional labor.* Emotional labor is tiring. In fact, it can be exhausting. Because of it, being a service provider may mean that you not only become tired, but also listless, dejected, grouchy, impatient, and even clumsy.

At the end of a long work shift, your store of emotional energy may be totally or partially drained. In such a case, the first outward signs of being spent emotionally is either a flat or negative attitude. In the hospitality business, it is not unusual for emotional energy to be lost through customer contact overload. In fact, *contact-overload syndrome* is a major contributor to less than stellar customer service attitudes exhibited by many service providers. The first service encounter of the day is generally quite different from the last, especially when we are talking about hundreds, if not thousands, of customer contacts. Spent emotional energy via customer contact overload remains a potent occupational hazard within the hospitality industry. The first step in combating it is to recognize that it exists and second to take appropriate steps to minimize it.

FROM THE QUALITY SERVICE HALL OF FAME

Attitudes are indeed infectious. In Surf City, U.S.A., there is a restaurant on the pier where this is evident. It is obvious by observing the energized service team that everybody likes working there. The entire crew not only shares an uncompromising friendly attitude, but also all the customers seem to catch it as well. There is a positive spirit and enthusiasm that permeates the whole place—all day long. I overheard one passionate customer extol, "Dude, this is truly one awesome place."

Attitudes Are Contagious

Like a fire spreads through dry brush, attitudes are caught from one person to another. Everyone on a hospitality service team is vulnerable. It takes just one person—one spark—and the entire service team is infected. I call this person the *attitude catalyst.* If that person is a supervisor or manager, attitudes spread particularly quick with plenty of fuel behind them. But a fellow service provider can also be an attitude catalyst with similar effects. The very nature of attitudes allows them to spread easily regardless of the source.

This spreading influence can work in one of two ways: toward the negative or toward the positive. When that pivotal person—the attitude catalyst—comes to work in a bad mood, or demonstrates any form of negativity, the entire service provider team is soon scowling, looking gloomy, tense, or otherwise uptight and troubled. Quality service naturally and inextricably suffers. The moment of truth is lost. Quality service goes down the drain and everybody loses—customers and service providers alike. In contrast, when the attitude catalyst comes to work in an upbeat mood and positive attitude, it does not take long for others to be likewise infected. When this happens, the service team soon becomes a bouquet of smiles. It becomes energized, cheerful, and exhilarated. The service team generates a healthy and vital customer service climate and its customers reap the benefits. In this scenario, quality service thrives. Both customers and service providers end up winning—all as a result of the contagious nature of positive attitudes. This occurs most readily when each and every service provider in any given hospitality service team has accepted the responsibility for being a positive attitude catalyst.

C hapter 12 in Review

KEY POINTS

1. The attitudes shown by hospitality service providers toward customers contribute directly to the quality of service provided.

2. Attitudes are conveyed to others by way of body language and tone of voice.

3. Spent emotional labor and customer contact overload can contribute to attitude metamorphosis.

4. Within any hospitality service team, attitudes are easily transferred from one person to the next.

KEY TERMS

Attitude catalyst
Attitude metamorphosis
Body language
Contact-overload syndrome
Emotional labor

STUDY QUESTIONS/DISCUSSION STIMULATORS

1. Why are positive attitudes vital to providing quality customer service?

2. What body language do you believe is most important when providing service? Why?

3. How does proper grooming reflect attitude?

4. How would you describe the best tone of voice for a hospitality setting?

5. How can attitudes change over time when providing customer service?

6. What are some ways attitude metamorphosis can be avoided?

7. How do attitudes among service providers become contagious?

8. What examples can you cite of a work group being infected by negative attitudes? By positive attitudes?

APPLICATION INTERACTION EXERCISE 20

ATTITUDES REFLECTED REFLECT THE REAL YOU

1. Based on your experience as a hospitality customer or service provider, describe the overall attitude that service providers should convey in a hospitality operation. This should be a general statement. We'll get more specific in a minute.

   _____

   _____

2. Based on what you have written in response to question #1, what specific body language would reflect this attitude?

   Facial expressions?

   _____

   Hand and body movements?

   _____

   Grooming standards?

   _____

3. Don't forget tone of voice. How would you describe the most desirable tone of voice that hospitality service providers should convey?

   _____

   _____

4. If you have worked or are working as a service provider, what is your organization doing to help service providers maintain a positive attitude throughout their shift?

   _____

   _____

5. What additional actions would you recommend?

   _____

   _____

APPLICATION INTERACTION EXERCISE 21

BODY LANGUAGE ANYONE?

Four sets of opposite nonverbal messages are presented below. Can you describe the possible messages these forms of body language send to customers?

Positive Messages

Face is relaxed and under control.
This communicates:

_____

_____

_____

Smile is natural and comfortable.
This communicates:

_____

_____

_____

Eye contact is maintained when talking and listening to others.
This communicates:

_____

_____

_____

Body movement is relaxed, yet deliberate and controlled.
This communicates:

_____

_____

_____

Negative Messages

Face is anxious and uptight.
This communicates:

_____

_____

_____

Smile is missing or forced.
This communicates:

_____

_____

_____

Eye contact is avoided when talking and listening.
This communicates:

_____

_____

_____

Body movement is harried and rushed.
This communicates:

_____

_____

_____

APPLICATION INTERACTION EXERCISE 22

HANDLING CONTACT OVERLOAD

We all need our batteries charged from time to time. Your ability to reenergize yourself is important to maintaining a positive attitude toward your customers.

Maintaining your positive attitude is your key to delivering quality customer service every minute on the job.

With these two factors in mind, answer the following questions.

1. Is contact overload syndrome a potential problem for you?

_____ Yes   _____ No

If so, how?

_____

_____

_____

_____

_____

_____

2. When you are emotionally tired, what can you do to reenergize yourself?

_____

_____

_____

_____

_____

_____

_____

_____

_____

_____

_____

13

Words That Sting— Words That Soothe

In addition to broadcasting our attitudes through our tone of voice and body language, the actual words that we use with guests also reveal a great deal about our ability to provide quality customer service. A service provider's tact when greeting a guest, when providing service, when making helpful suggestions, or when handling a problem or concern are all dependent in part on the manner in which sentences are phrased and words used. The ability to say the right thing at the right time in the right way is the essence of quality verbal communication.

FROM THE QUALITY SERVICE HALL OF SHAME

A sign placed in the bathroom of a small hotel read: "Please notify desk if for any reason you wish to remove any towels or linen from the premises. Our linens are impregnated with a magnetic yarn that will set off security devices."

A food server pouring coffee for a group of four women noticed that one of them kept her hands under the table. He commented, "What's the matter? Don't you have any hands?" She lifted her arms, exposing two artificial hands.

A large man (over 300 pounds) had just finished his dinner at a local steak house when the food server walked up and said, "Boy, you really pigged that down, didn't you." Later, the server couldn't understand why the customer complained to the manager.

Tactful Language

As a hospitality service provider, what you say to customers should be appropriate to the situation. For example, some hospitality environments are more formal whereas others tend to be more informal. The appropriateness of the language used in each setting will differ. Regardless of the setting, however, no customer should needlessly be put off by improper grammar or poor use of language. Appropriateness of words goes beyond mere grammar, however. To be appropriate, verbal communication must also be tactful and inoffensive. Moreover, the communication should contribute to customer enjoyment, relaxation, and feelings of hospitality. Customers should never be made to feel uncomfortable or embarrassed by a careless, callous, or otherwise stupid comment from anyone in the operation. Polite words such as "please," "I'm sorry," or "thank you" are always tactful. They should be used openly in an unlimited way. Deciding what is tactful and what isn't requires a particular level of sensitivity on the part of the service provider.

Naming Names

Calling customers by name is always appropriate. Yet, using a guest's name at the right time and in the right way is a hospitality skill that customers generally expect but rarely receive. The use of customer names reflects a special caring for customers. It communicates respect for them as individuals. That is why hospitality service providers need to use customer names as much as possible. Calling customers by name is a fundamental verbal skill. It is also great hospitality, for it reflects an appreciation for the personal side of quality service. When service providers speak to a customer by name, they clearly show they are attempting to relate to that customer personally.

FROM THE QUALITY SERVICE HALL OF FAME

One California restaurant company known for its restaurants with a view has its hosts write down each party's name upon arrival. When the table is ready, the host personally locates the party (no overhead paging system is used) and always refers to them by name: "Mr. Jackson, your table is now ready."

Another California restaurant chain uses a card system to phonetically spell customer's names. When customers check in at the front desk, the host writes the name down on a card and places it in a designated location where the table server can pick it up and refer to it.

A major Asian air carrier requires all cabin crew attendants in business and first-class sections to call passengers by name during all service encounters. To facilitate this, a diagram of the seats in the cabin with passengers' names recorded on each seat is posted as an easy reference for the crew.

TWO INGREDIENTS

Hospitality service providers need two internal ingredients to bring this guest expectation to life on a regular basis. First, you need a system for obtaining and recording guest names. Second, once you have the name, you need to use it in front of the guest. Common ways of obtaining guest names in advance are:

- Reservations

- Bookings

- Waiting lists

- Ticket sales

Means of acquiring guest names at the time of service interaction include credit cards and written service requests. Of course, the old-fashioned strategy of merely asking the guest what his or her name is remains a fruitful option. But, each of these strategies will have little impact on the level of service unless guest names are actually used. Many hotel operations expect their front desk representative to use the guest's name at least three times during the check-in process. One restaurant chain expects every customer who pays with a credit card to be thanked by name when the card is returned. Unfortunately for hospitality consumers, these occurrences remain the exception rather than the rule.

Chapter 13 in Review

KEY CONCEPTS

1. The actual words used by service providers reveal a great deal about their ability to provide quality customer service.

2. The words spoken by hospitality service providers should be appropriate and tactful.

3. Referring to a customer by name during the service encounter is a quality service plus.

4. Effectively naming names requires a system of obtaining guest names and for the service provider to actually speak the name during the service encounter.

KEY TERMS

Naming names
Tactful language

STUDY QUESTIONS/DISCUSSION STIMULATORS

1. Should a hospitality service provider use slang or jargon during a service encounter? Why or why not?

2. How does proper grammar contribute to a quality service encounter?

3. How can talking too fast adversely affect a service encounter?

4. Why does naming names remain a less than common occurrence in many hospitality operations?

APPLICATION INTERACTION EXERCISE 23

CHOOSING TACTFUL WORDS

1. From your experience as a service provider or a hospitality customer, what polite phrases or words should hospitality service providers be using? List them here.

   _____

   _____

   _____

   _____

2. What phrases or words should hospitality service providers avoid? List a few of them here.

   _____

   _____

   _____

   _____

3. What topics of conversation are **acceptable** for hospitality service providers?

   _____

   _____

   _____

   _____

4. What topics of conversation are **unacceptable**?

   _____

   _____

   _____

   _____

14

The Joy of Surprises—
Providing the Unexpected

Providing a level of service that is unexpected but very gratifying to the customer requires perceiving what customers need and want in a special way. Why? Because this level of service goes beyond the procedural components of timeliness, accommodation, and anticipation in that it requires service providers to "tune-in" to customers as human beings. It requires them to "read" the customer and to establish rapport between the customer and themselves, to be sensitive to the four basic customer service needs. I call this component of quality service *attentiveness*. Attentiveness embodies empathy, an understanding of customer feelings, wants, and desires. Even though all customers come to hospitality establishments with the four basic customer service needs, many come with additional and varied expectations, wants, and needs. Attentive service providers attempt to identify these needs and do their best to meet them.

R eading the Guest

Reading the guest requires being sensitive to guests' nonverbal and verbal *cues*, of which they may not even be aware. Catching these cues helps the service provider to be aware of a customer's particular need. This can happen without the guest saying a word. Common cues often picked up by experienced service providers include—

- The customer's age

- His or her attire

- The group mix of which the guest is a part

- Guest body language

- Verbal abilities as well as his or her tone of voice

Each of these provides vital signs that the observant service provider can use to provide service that is not only customized but also special.

FROM THE QUALITY SERVICE HALL OF FAME

A little girl was crying in the lobby of a hotel across from Disneyland. Her mother explained to a service associate that she had inadvertently left a shopping bag containing a stuffed Goofy for her little girl at the tram stop. The service associate was just getting off his shift so he said that he would go back to the tram stop before he left and look for the bag. He did, but to no avail. The bag was gone and the stuffed Goofy was nowhere to be found—much to the little girl's dismay. A while later, the service associate proposed a plan to his supervisor. By 7:00 that evening a new stuffed Goofy was sent up to the little girl's room, compliments of the hotel.

R apport

Rapport embodies the attitudes, feelings, and relationships that help establish mutual respect between customers and service providers. It establishes a friendly relationship. Customers are made to feel comfortable and relaxed. They feel the server genuinely has their interest at heart.

Without rapport, effective communication breaks down, and service quality suffers. A lack of rapport shows in a service provider who is overly pompous, condescending, antagonistic, or in some way irritating. It also shows when the service provider fails to take the time to understand customer needs and desires. Regardless of the cause, customers feel alienated from or intimidated by service providers when rapport is missing. Rapport does not necessarily guarantee quality service, but a lack of it most certainly leads to a nonquality experience for the customer.

E mpathy

Empathy is the epitome of understanding other people—putting yourself in their position, seeing through their eyes, and walking in their shoes. Service providers with strong personal skills are empathetic. Ask yourself, *"If I were this customer, what would I want, and how would I like to be treated?"* Increased empathy on the part of service providers leads to a higher level of personal service. This is not to say that you need to know all about your customers. That is neither possible, nor desirable. Yet, hospitality customers do expect service providers to empathize on some level with their needs and wants.

FROM THE QUALITY SERVICE HALL OF SHAME

A woman ran up to the fast-food service counter and said, "I need a cup of water. My husband is choking." The counter person responded with a wide smile, "Would you like a large or a small?"

Tuning-in

Tuning-in to guest's feelings leads to higher levels of attentive service. This special service skill is evident when you do something nice for guests—something not necessarily required of your job, but something you do nevertheless. This is often referred to as "wowing" the guest. It means exhibiting a special degree of thoughtfulness. It also means being particularly sensitive to common customer cues. I have listed six of these cues. Following each cue I provide a few examples of how an attentive hospitality service provider could possibly respond.

CUE #1: CUSTOMER AGE

- Small children may need extra napkins, small glasses or extra glasses, high chairs, extra beds, or other accommodations, or other items or activities.

- Teens are into unusual and fun experiences that are reasonably priced.

- Young adults enjoy specialty items and an active, informal environment.

- Older adults appreciate polite, more traditional approaches to service and like to be shown deference.

- Seniors look for economy and a special helping hand. They are less tolerant of waiting and, many times, enjoy a friendly conversation.

CUE #2: ATTIRE

- Customers dressed in casual attire are usually out to have a good time and enjoy themselves in a relaxed, informal way.

- A business suit can often mean this is a "working" person who would appreciate efficient and unobtrusive service.

- Formal attire may mean a special celebration that can be enhanced by special service or may mean the guest is on the way to another event and hence may have time constraints.

CUE #3: GROUP MIX

- Groups like special attention. Understanding service providers find out who they are and what type of group they represent.

- A same-sex group is usually less inhibited than mixed groups and looks for service that matches its informality.

- With family groups, the sensitive service provider will defer to the senior member of the family and provide for the needs of any children.

- An attentive service provider will provide unobtrusive, efficient service to business-oriented groups.

CUE #4: BODY LANGUAGE

- When arms are folded or noses or chins are being stroked, customers are tired of waiting. Or they may be looking at their watches, or looking around.

- When customers are looking around, a sensitive service provider assumes they are looking for him or her.

- In restaurants, closed menus usually mean customers are ready to order.

CUE #5: VERBAL ABILITIES

- When customers are extremely fluent, the smart service provider will show deference and respect.

- When customers are less fluent, the smart service provider shows patience, respect, and understanding. Procedures and options are also explained slowly and carefully.

- When customers are new to or unfamiliar with the property, the attentive service provider offers special help or suggestions. The customers are set at ease.

CUE #6: TONE OF VOICE

- Customers' tone of voice can tell the tuned-in service provider whether the guests are relaxed and having a good time, or whether they are uptight, hurried, or annoyed.

- The sensitive service provider listens not only to what customers are saying but also how they are saying it, and they respond accordingly.

Chapter 14 in Review

KEY CONCEPTS

1. Going beyond customer expectations is an important component of quality customer service.

2. The ability to read guests, establish rapport, and empathize with them are the keys to providing attentive customer service.

KEY TERMS

Attentiveness
Empathy
Rapport
Reading the guest

STUDY QUESTIONS/DISCUSSION STIMULATORS

1. How does providing attentive service contribute to the level of service provided?

2. What skills are necessary to read the guest?

3. Why is the establishment of rapport with guests an important foundation for attentive customer service?

4. What role does empathy play in a service provider's ability to render quality customer service?

APPLICATION INTERACTION EXERCISE 24

"WOWING" THE GUEST

1. As a hospitality service provider, or potential service provider, what are several ways you can provide **unexpected** and/or **special** service to guests? List a few ideas here.

_____

_____

_____

2. How can you "tune-in" or be more sensitive to guest needs?

_____

Tell about a time from your experience when you or another service provider did this.

_____

_____

_____

3. How can service providers establish a greater rapport with guests?

_____

Tell about a time from your experience when a service provider did this.

_____

_____

_____

4. How can service providers develop greater empathy for guests?

_____

Tell about a time from your experience when a service provider did this.

_____

_____

_____

15

Lending a Helping Hand

Hospitality consumers want and expect helpful, knowledgeable assistance when they need it. When they are purchasing something with which they are not totally familiar, customers seek advice. They refrain from buying a car from a person who can't discuss the advantages and disadvantages of a turbocharger or explain why a sixteen-valve engine is superior to the eight-valve variety. They don't purchase insurance from someone who is unable to explain the difference between term and whole-life policies. Consumers want their service representatives to be knowledgeable about the products they are selling. This is particularly true for hospitality service providers.

Product Knowledge

As a front desk representative, one of your jobs is to sell your property to guests. That is why you need to be well versed in all the features and benefits of the property. Customers expect nothing less. As a food service provider selling and serving wine, you also need to know the wine list. Similarly, if you are selling and serving dinners, you need to know the menu selections backward and forward, how items are prepared, what they look like, and how they taste. The same principle applies for *all* hospitality products, regardless of the setting, location, or market.

FROM THE QUALITY SERVICE HALL OF SHAME

One frustrated diner related what happened to him at a Santa Barbara restaurant. "I asked the server if she had a wine to recommend. Her response was, 'What do you like?' When it came time to order our entrées I asked her if she had a recommendation. She answered, 'Everything is good.' When I asked her whether the Seafood Jambalaya contained any meat, she said that it didn't. Being a vegetarian, I ordered it. When the jambalaya was served, I noticed that it had slices of sausage in it. I asked her about the sausage. She said, 'Oh, that's not meat. That's sausage. I thought you meant meat meat.' All I could do was shake my head and ask for another glass of wine."

Assisting the Guest

Product knowledge goes hand in hand with the ability to assist a customer making a decision. Restaurant customers often want assistance in making a menu choice; hotel guests, a room choice; and travel customers, a destination site. The need for assistance is particularly acute for first-time customers, but when they receive a response from a service provider such as, "Everything is good," or "I really can't say," or "I'm not into that, myself," there lies a great discrepancy between the guidance they are receiving and the guidance they want.

FROM THE QUALITY SERVICE HALL OF FAME

A frequent traveler commented, "I travel a lot because of my job as a sales representative. I have discovered some great restaurants in each of my assigned cities thanks to the suggestions of the front-desk clerks in the hotels where I stay. It's almost kind of a game. Each time I check in, I ask them to recommend a different type of restaurant. One time it will be Italian, another time Thai, another time Greek, and so on. They really think it's great. I believe that they actually anticipate my arrival and get ready for the next restaurant challenge. Over the years I have ended up in some great restaurants—places that I would never have found on my own and far better than most of the restaurants suggested in the hotel's dining selections booklet left in each room."

The Five Forbidden Phrases

As a hospitality service provider, you would be wise to become acquainted with the five forbidden phrases, so that you can erase them entirely from your verbal repertoire. The five forbidden phrases are:

1. I don't know.

2. We can't do that.

3. You'll have to . . .

4. Hang on a second. I'll be right back.

5. Saying "no" at the beginning of a sentence.

Each of these remarks reflects, in its own distinctive way, a general lack of willingness to be of assistance to guests. Quality service requires that service providers avoid them, and instead, choose positive alternatives (as shown in Figure 15.1).

FIGURE **15.1**

The Five Forbidden Phrases

Phrases to Avoid	*Positive Helpful Options*
I don't know.	I will find out.
We can't do that.	What I can do is . . .
You'll have to . . .	May I help you to . . .
Hang on a second. I'll be right back.	May I call you back in a few minutes.
No.	Yes.

To better understand why the positive helpful options are preferable responses, let's take a closer at each of the five forbidden phrases.

"I don't know." The biggest problem with saying, "I don't know," is that it is negative. It is not a problem because you don't know. Being a hospitality service provider is a continuous learning experience. There will always be situations and/or questions from customers that stymie you. This is inevitable. So, what can you do? What you can do is always attempt to respond with a positive statement rather than a negative one. When unsure of how to respond or what to do, the positive approach would be to say something like, "Let me find out" or "I'd like to check on this" or "I'll find out." Remember, a positive response is always better than a negative one.

"We can't do that." This reflects another type of negative response. By being negative, it fails to establish a helpful relationship with your customer. Saying, "We can't do that" is equivalent to slamming a door in the face of a guest. It's a communication stopper. It doesn't lead to a solution or helpful alternatives. As I discussed in the chapter on accommodation, as a service provider customers will invariably ask you to do some things that you simply are unable to do. The key to providing quality service lies in your response. Once again, choose the positive option. Talk about what you *can* do, not what you can't.

"You'll have to . . ." Beginning a sentence with "you," referring to your customer, puts the onus of responsibility on the guest for whatever needs to occur and away from you, the service provider. Therefore, because of its basic approach, starting a statement with this phrase fails to be helpful. It makes the customer the problem solver rather than you. In addition, using this phrase

tends to put a sense of blame or fault onto the customer. There is an implication that the customer has done something incorrectly. Even when the customer has in fact blundered, such implications should be avoided whenever possible. More helpful alternatives would be to say, "I recommend . . ." or "Some guests have . . ." or "May I assist you to . . ."

"Hang on a second. I'll be right back." The problem with this statement is that it usually ends up being a lie. Whether on the telephone or face to face, it is better to be accurate in the estimated time you will be able to return and be of assistance. If you need several minutes, say so. If you think that you may even be longer and you are on the telephone, always offer to call the person back. And, of course, always apologize for having the customer wait for your assistance for any extended periods. The second problem with this phrase is saying, "Hang on." Such a comment represents inappropriate slang. It also implies that the guest is being impatient. It would be more polite and helpful to say something like, "I'll be right with you in a minute or two" or "Can I call you back?" or "This may take some time, please bear with me."

"No" at the beginning of a sentence. This is the biggest no-no of the forbidden five. If saying, "We can't do that" is slamming a door in front of the customer, beginning a sentence with "no" is equivalent to putting up a brick wall between you and the customer. Saying this is blatantly negative, right from the start. It immediately terminates all further discussion. Moreover, it suggests that the guest is wrong or mistaken. In short, I recommend to all hospitality service providers to never say "no" to guests. Instead, always say something positive. When you have to deny a customer, respond with, "I'm sorry." Then proceed to tell what you can and will do. After all, that is what helping the customer is all about.

Chapter 15 in Review

KEY CONCEPTS

1. Hospitality customers want and expect help in making decisions in areas where they are unfamiliar or unsure.

2. The ability to help guests requires product knowledge on the part of the service provider.

3. Helping the guest requires a positive approach, avoiding the five forbidden phrases.

KEY TERMS

Assisting the guest
Product knowledge
The five forbidden phrases

STUDY QUESTIONS/DISCUSSION STIMULATORS

1. Why is product knowledge crucial to the ability of service providers to assist guests?

2. Under what circumstances will guests most likely want or need assistance in making a hospitality choice?

3. What is wrong with using each of the five forbidden phrases? What makes the suggested alternatives better?

APPLICATION INTERACTION EXERCISE 25

HELPING THE GUEST

List below at least ten different ways service providers can provide guidance for guests in a typical hospitality organization.

1.

2.

3.

4.

5.

6.

7.

8.

9.

10.

16

Selling That Sells

As with any business, the hospitality business depends on sales for survival and success. Without sales, there would be no business. Therefore, it is inappropriate to view service as an end in itself. However intangible, service is as much a product as food and rooms. Yet it is a product that serves a special function. That function is to cultivate, facilitate, and accumulate sales. Service is a means, not an end. If it fails to provide the means to sales, the hospitality organization suffers the consequences.

Service as a Means to Building Sales

Once we begin to view service as a means of building hospitality sales, our perspective of quality service and its evaluation changes greatly. Traditionally, a restaurant food server's job was viewed as one of taking orders and delivering food. Similarly, a front desk representative's job was often seen as primarily checking guests in and checking them out. Yet, today's food and beverage servers as well as hotel front desk representatives need to be viewed, first and foremost, as sales representatives for their respective operations. Department stores have sales associates, and insurance companies have sales representatives. Most businesses use a sales force in one form or another to sell goods and services. The same is true for the hospitality industry.

Selling Skill Requirements

As with the other components of the personal dimension of quality service, effective selling skills require an understanding and appreciation of the human dynamic. They require rapport between seller and customer. They also require a degree of empathy on the part of the seller, so the seller can understand and meet the customer's needs and wants. These are basic principles upon which all personal selling is based. In short, hospitality sales require human-relation skills on the part of the seller. These skills include:

- *Adopting a sales perspective* to the job assuming that you can sell

- *Expanding the awareness* of guests as to what products or services are available

- Explaining the *features* of what you are selling

- Describing the *benefits* of what you are selling

Let's take a closer look at each of these important hospitality service provider skills.

ADOPTING A SALES PERSPECTIVE

This is the first requirement of an effective sales person. You have to be willing to step up to the challenge of selling. This means not only accepting it but also embracing it. It also means being open to learning and willing to improve your selling techniques. Additionally, it is important that you view the development of selling skills as an integral part of your job, not an extra extension of it. To make this step easier, many hospitality service providers choose personal favorite products or services so their approach to selling these items is genuine and sincere.

EXPANDING YOUR CUSTOMERS' AWARENESS

Effective selling involves letting your customers know what is available. This is the information-sharing stage of effective selling. Guests may not be fully aware of the many options available to them. This is your opportunity to help them become fully informed so they can make an informed consumer choice. Many customers prefer to hear options orally rather than to read about them. Often available options are simply not printed for guests to read so the only way to let your customers know about these available products or services is to tell about them. Such items often include restaurant daily specials, special room rates, and travel fares.

FROM THE QUALITY SERVICE HALL OF FAME

A memorable line from a food server to a dining customer: "There's one piece of cheesecake left, and it's calling your name."

One notable food server's secret to successful selling was to have a favorite in each menu category. He had a favorite wine, a favorite chicken, beef, fish, and pasta dish, and so on. He would never recommend or try to sell the most expensive item on the menu fearing that if he did so his credibility would be lost. Although his favorites were not the most expensive, he could describe them with real enthusiasm. All his customers appreciated his genuineness. Plus, he received far more tips than any other of his fellow servers.

EXPLAINING THE FEATURES

Here is another area of quality service where your product knowledge kicks in. You have to be fully informed and up to date about what it is that you are selling so you can pass that information on to your guests. In addition, effective salespeople are good at using expressive descriptive words when telling about a particular product or service. For example, a chocolate sauce can be described as "dark and rich," or a beverage as "smooth and light." A guest room can be described as "light and airy with a great view." Regardless of the descriptors that you choose, it is important to be enthusiastic and genuine in your approach.

DESCRIBING THE BENEFITS

There are always benefits to purchasing every hospitality product or service. Sometimes these benefits are not self-apparent. This means effective salespeople are sure to always cite a benefit or two of any products that they are selling. This is the time for your positive attitude to kick in. Always accentuate the positive. This means always having something good to say about what you are selling. An effective explanation of benefits doesn't have to be a long, drawn-out affair. Often a few words can do the job. Here are some common examples:

- "You'll love it."

- "It tastes great."

- "We're getting lots of compliments about it tonight."

- "It's well worth it."

- "It's a great value."

- "It's huge, enough for two."

- "If you haven't tried one yet, you have to have one."

- "It's very comfortable."

- "Guests love it."

- "Good choice."

FROM THE QUALITY SERVICE HALL OF FAME

A supervisor noted that one of her front desk clerks was particularly enthusiastic about the hotel. While checking in guests, she would always mention the services and special activities available in the hotel. When asked to share her approach at a training session, the clerk said, "There are so many exciting things going on here; I just think it would be a shame for our guests not to take advantage of them."

Selling a Total Experience

What we are selling in hospitality organizations is different from the product in most other sales-oriented operations. Although a clothing store sells clothes and an auto dealership sells cars, hospitality organizations sell much more than food, rooms, or travel connections. They also sell value, convenience, safety, atmosphere, fun, and excitement. In short, they sell a *total experience*. And the level of personal service exhibited by service providers molds that experience. When a hospitality service provider approaches selling from this perspective, the meaning of selling skills (i.e., salesmanship) takes on a whole new definition and function.

From a customer's perspective, effective selling requires respect, tact, consideration, and caring, i.e., a personal approach. It also requires knowledge and assistance on the part of the sales team. Hospitality consumers don't want pushy, obnoxious, affronting individuals serving them. They don't appreciate this kind of selling in other businesses, so why should they tolerate it in a hospitality setting? They expect and should receive tactful, friendly, and knowledgeable assistance whenever they make a hospitality purchase. Anytime hospitality is consumed, the consumers should feel that their money has been well spent. In addition, they should feel that they have been treated with respect and courtesy. Skillful selling and quality service, after all, are one and the same.

Chapter 16 in Review

KEY CONCEPTS

1. Customer service is a means to cultivate, facilitate, and accumulate sales.

2. The job of providing service should be viewed as one of generating sales.

3. The four selling skills service providers need to develop are assuming you can sell, expanding your guests' awareness, explaining features of what you are selling, and describing the benefits of making a purchase.

4. Hospitality organizations are selling a total experience.

KEY TERMS

Expanding awareness
Product features
Product benefits
Sales perspective
Total experience

STUDY QUESTIONS/DISCUSSION STIMULATORS

1. Why should quality customer service be viewed as a means rather than an end?

2. Why is it important for a hospitality service provider to adopt a sales perspective?

3. Why is it important to expand a guest's awareness of what is available?

4. Why is explaining a product's features and benefits a vital component of effective selling?

APPLICATION INTERACTION EXERCISE 26

SELLING SKILLS

1. What products and/or services are sold by a typical hospitality organization? List them here.

   _____

   _____

   _____

2. How could guests be made more aware of the items you have listed in #1?

   _____

   _____

   _____

3. Do service providers have an opportunity to upgrade guest choices? If so, how?

   _____

   _____

   _____

4. Choose a particular hospitality product or service to sell. Name it here:

   _____

   What descriptive words could you use to sell this item?

   _____

   _____

   _____

5. From your experience as a hospitality customer, how could the selling skills of service providers be improved?

   _____

   _____

   _____

   _____

APPLICATION INTERACTION EXERCISE 27

DESCRIBING FEATURES AND BENEFITS

In the left-hand column, list up to eight typical products and/or services sold in hospitality organizations.

For each product or service listed write down a few features and benefits of each that would help a service provider effectively sell that particular item.

Service/Product	Features	Benefits
_____	_____	_____
	_____	_____
	_____	_____
_____	_____	_____
	_____	_____
	_____	_____
_____	_____	_____
	_____	_____
	_____	_____
_____	_____	_____
	_____	_____
	_____	_____
_____	_____	_____
	_____	_____
	_____	_____
_____	_____	_____
	_____	_____
	_____	_____
_____	_____	_____
	_____	_____
	_____	_____
_____	_____	_____
	_____	_____
	_____	_____

17

The Challenge of Gracious Problem Solving

The ability to graciously solve customer-related problems is the ultimate test of quality service. This significant ingredient of service incorporates the entire package of customer expectations in the personal dimension. It requires finely tuned attitudes, verbal competencies, and behavior skills on the part of the service provider. Customers expect problems to be handled not only expeditiously, but also smoothly, calmly, and tactfully. They want to know they have been heard and what the follow-up action will be. They want their problems handled in a positive way, with appropriate apologies when necessary. Most important, they want the problem to be acknowledged and dealt with.

This is certainly the time to remember the four basic customer service needs. When there is a problem, it becomes more imperative than ever for you to understand and respect customers because they are choosing to do business with you. Providing for each of the four basic customer service needs is the important first step in mutually solving a problem with a guest. These four basic needs remain—

1. The need to be understood

2. The need to feel welcome

3. The need for comfort

4. The need to feel important

These customer-based needs serve as the conceptual base for the five problem-solving imperatives.

FROM THE QUALITY SERVICE HALL OF SHAME

I ordered a swordfish steak at a local seafood restaurant. When it was served, I noticed that it had only been grilled on one side. I pointed this out to the server. Without a word of apology, he swooped up the plate and left. About ten minutes later he returned with my plate. He said something clever like, "Here's your swordfish. Hope it's okay this time." Then he was off, not waiting for a response. The fish was now cooked on both sides. A little more rice pilaf had also been added to the plate—possibly to somehow make up for the oversight.

The Five Problem-Solving Imperatives

With the basic customer service needs serving as the foundation for successfully solving customer-related problems, gracious problem solving can occur when the five problem-solving imperatives are followed. From a customer's perspective, gracious problem solving is most likely to occur when you, the service provider—

1. Listen and repeat

2. Acknowledge

3. Apologize

4. Agree

5. Thank

That's a summary of what you need to do when a customer complains. Now, of course, I need to explain these five imperatives so you can, first, understand the rationale behind each one, and second, begin to adopt them as part and parcel of your quality service skill repertoire. Let's take them one at a time.

LISTEN AND REPEAT

The first step in dealing with a guest complaint is to listen carefully to what the complaint actually is. Make sure you understand it fully and then repeat what you have heard back to the customer. Repeating what you have heard back provides verification that you know exactly what the nature of the complaint is and what is involved. It also lets the customer know that the complaint has been accurately communicated.

ACKNOWLEDGE

This step involves acknowledging the guest's feelings, such as anger, frustration, or disappointment. Here is where understanding and empathy kick in. Use it. For example, you can say, "I understand how you feel" or "This would make me upset too." When you acknowledge the customer's feelings, you are not only expressing openness to his or her plight, but you are also establishing a nondefensive approach to solving the problem. This approach tends to set the customer at ease because you have expressed your understanding and support.

APOLOGIZE

Once you know what the problem is and how the guest is feeling, it is time to say you are sorry. Even if you personally have done nothing that has led to or caused the complaint, it is important to apologize anyway. Apologize to the guest for being put into such a situation—regardless of the reasons or responsible party.

AGREE

This step reflects a two-way problem-solving process. Get the guest involved in deciding how the problem can best be resolved. You can ask how he or she would like the problem resolved, or you may suggest a particular solution. Either way or both, it is important to agree on a solution together. By doing this, you direct your energies and those of the customer toward constructive solutions and problem solving rather than harping on the problem or casting blame. It also goes a long way to calm or otherwise win over an angry guest.

THANK

Always thank the guest for complaining. Why? Because without hearing the complaint you may continue totally unaware that a problem exists. And when you are unaware of a problem, you can do nothing to prevent or minimize it. That is why any time a customer complains, that customer is doing you a big favor. The complaint serves to make you a more alert and knowledgeable service provider. Knowing about the complaint, you can now do something about it, and, more important, you can help prevent such situations from occurring again. Customer complaints serve as invaluable feedback to hospitality service providers. That deserves a big "Thank you."

FROM THE QUALITY SERVICE HALL OF FAME

We arrived late in the afternoon at LAX on a flight from Denver. My kids and I proceeded directly to the baggage claim area. Our personal bags arrived, but our skis and snowboards failed to appear. The kids watched our luggage while I volunteered to walk down to the service desk. The woman at the service desk appeared to be exhausted, but very nice nonetheless. She tried to track down the missing skis and boards, but without any luck. She suggested that we wait for the next flight from Denver to arrive. The wait would be about thirty minutes. My son was greatly on edge because he had another snowboard trip to Lake Tahoe scheduled for the very next day. The woman at the service desk offered to have all the missing pieces delivered to our home addresses no later than the next day. That time frame, however, would not work for my son. He got a little testy with the woman. Our only option at this point was to wait for the next flight to arrive. Much to our mutual relief, all boards and skis appeared in the special area for oversized luggage. We left the airport tired, relieved, and with a fist full of airline discount certificates pleasantly supplied by the tired but helpful airline service representative.

Customer Compensation

The goal of gracious problem solving is to have the guest leave happy or otherwise satisfied with the solution to the problem. That is why it is vital to involve the customer in the determination of a solution. This generally involves a *customer compensation* of some sort. When something has happened to guests that shouldn't have happened, they need to be compensated in some way whether it is compensation for a night's lodging, a meal, or a future ticket, room, or meal. This is the area where the service provider needs to use experience, discretion, and common sense as a guide. There are no pat or formula answers to the appropriate amount of compensation to a guest who has experienced a problem. That is why it is always advisable to ask the guests how they would like the issue resolved. Remember gracious problem solving is a two-way process. If what the guest wants is impossible or unjustified by the very nature of the problem, the service provider needs to explain why the request cannot be granted and counter with what can be done. In most cases, from my experience, a mutually agreed-upon solution is the best. This is critical because if a disgruntled guest leaves the problem-solving process without feeling satisfied at some level, that guest will most likely choose a competitor the next time around.

Chapter 17 in Review

KEY CONCEPTS

1. Gracious guest problem solving is built on the foundation of the four basic customer service needs.

2. There are five steps to achieving gracious problem solving with customers.

3. Gracious problem solving usually involves some sort of customer compensation.

KEY TERMS

Customer compensation
Five problem-solving imperatives

STUDY QUESTIONS/DISCUSSION STIMULATORS

1. Why are the four basic customer service needs particularly important to fulfill when dealing with guest problems or complaints?

2. What is the purpose or reasoning behind each of the five problem-solving imperatives?

3. Why is some sort of customer compensation a vital ingredient when dealing with a customer problem or complaint?

APPLICATION INTERACTION EXERCISE 28

GRACIOUS PROBLEM SOLVING

1. From your experience as a hospitality customer or service provider, what could service providers do to improve how they deal with guest complaints and/or problems?

_____

_____

_____

2. What can service providers do to make sure the guest is **understood**?

_____

_____

_____

3. What can service providers do to make sure the guest **feels welcome**?

_____

_____

_____

4. What can service providers do to make sure the guest is **comfortable**?

_____

_____

_____

5. What can service providers do to make sure the guest **feels important**?

_____

_____

_____

APPLICATION INTERACTION EXERCISE 29

RESPONDING TO CUSTOMER COMPLAINTS OR PROBLEMS

List below the most common complaints and/or problems that guests tend to bring to hospitality service providers. After each item on your list, indicate what the appropriate service provider response should be.

Common Complaint and/or Problem   *Appropriate Response(s)*

1.

2.

3.

4.

5.

6.

7.

8.

9.

10.

APPLICATION INTERACTION EXERCISE 30

THE CASE OF THE COMPLAINING CUSTOMER

You are the hostess at a nice full-service restaurant that takes reservations. A guest approaches the desk and says that his name is Jones and that he has a seven o'clock reservation. You look at your reservations list and find nothing for Jones at seven or at any time the rest of the evening. You inform him that you can't find his reservation. In a very huffy way, he informs you that this is the second time this has happened to him at this restaurant and that he called just yesterday at three in the afternoon for today's reservation. He is getting more and more angry and indicates that he wants immediate action.

Write out your response below.

First I would say: _____

_____

Then, I would repeat the complaint by saying _____

_____

Next, I would acknowledge feelings by saying _____

_____

I would apologize by saying _____

_____

I would agree on a solution by saying _____

_____

Last, I would thank the guest by saying _____

_____

18

The Challenge of the Difficult Guest

A guest may be difficult because of a particular problem or complaint, but not necessarily. Guests may be difficult for many reasons, but they tend to have some characteristics in common. Believe it or not, most difficult guests are operating from a base of insecurity. One (or more) of the four basic customer service needs is lacking and crying for attention. Difficult customers are often merely expressing a need, although they may be choosing an inappropriate and impolite way of communicating it. It is important to remember that they are being difficult for their own reasons, not because of you. By working to meet these needs, you can go a long way toward being successful with a guest who is being troublesome or otherwise challenging.

Difficult guests come in all shapes, sizes, and varieties. Here are just a few examples:

- The demanding guest

- The nasty or obnoxious person

- The very particular or picky person

- The constant critic

- The nonstop talker

- The condescending guest

- The indecisive person

- The intoxicated individual

- The argumentative customer

- The person who just doesn't understand

- The rude or impolite guest

FROM THE QUALITY SERVICE HALL OF SHAME

A high-powered attorney was hosting a small get-together at a downtown eatery. After the group had consumed several bottles of wine, the host was not only getting particularly loud and demanding, but also making inappropriate and demeaning remarks to the female server. Clapping his hands high above his head, he exhorted, "We need more bread and more wine." When the server reached across the table to grab the empty breadbasket, she "accidentally" knocked the host's full glass of red wine into his lap. She then responded with a sly smile, "Oh, I'm so terribly sorry. Clumsy me."

Five Tips for Dealing with Difficult Customers

As you can see from the brief list, difficult guests can come in many different variations and forms. Dealing with them requires all the customer service skills you have to call upon—and sometimes more. With that in mind, here are five suggestions for helping you effectively confront these types of service encounters.

1. **Don't take it personally.** This is one of the hardest customer service skills to learn. Remember that difficult people are not attacking you personally (even though it may seem that they are).

2. **Remain calm. Listen carefully.** This is easy advice to give, but in practice very difficult to do. It may help to take a deep breath and plan your choice of word very carefully. Use your effective listening skills by repeating back what you have heard, paraphrasing the guest, making sure you have heard him/her correctly.

3. **Focus on the problem, not the person.** If possible, go to a quiet area. Sit down. Be a problem-solver. Try to figure out what this person needs, and satisfy this need in some way, if you can. Let the customer know what you can do—not what you can't do. Be positive.

4. **Reward yourself for turning a difficult customer into a happy one.** Smile. Pat yourself on the back. Know that you have accomplished an amazing feat. You are a customer service hero.

5. **When all else fails, ask for help.** When you find yourself confronted with a difficult situation that you don't know how to handle, involve your supervisor. Certain problems may require him/her to handle. If so, find out what these problem areas are, and observe how they are handled.

FROM THE QUALITY SERVICE HALL OF FAME

A celebrity was checking into a large hotel. He said to the service associate, "I need a wake up call at precisely six o'clock. If it's a minute late, I'm going to hold you personally responsible. I want dinner in my room at seven o'clock sharp. Got that? And breakfast at six-thirty on the nose—or else you are going to hear from me." The associate replied, "I'm sure we can do all of that, but let me have you talk with my manager to make sure we get everything just right." The manager then escorted the guest over to a cozy, more private section of the lobby where they could sit down. She recorded and verified all of his exact service needs for the next two days—which were delivered precisely as requested.

Cutting Your Losses

Sometimes hospitality service providers have to cut their losses. Unfortunately, you cannot please all guests all the time. There are instances when it becomes virtually impossible to please a guest. The important fact to remember, however, is that this is extremely rare. The vast majority of customer-related situations with difficult guests can, if handled correctly, generate mutually acceptable solutions for service providers and guests alike. Providing quality customer service is a numbers game. The more guests a service provider can satisfy the better. Remember that quality customer service requires consistency, not perfection. The key to achieving quality customer service is to overwhelmingly increase the number of service encounter successes and significantly reduce the number of service failures. After all, this is what gracious problem solving and dealing effectively with difficult guests is all about. And, as a result, when both you and your customers end up as winning, you have indeed achieved quality customer service.

Chapter 18 in Review

KEY CONCEPTS

1. Many difficult guests are operating from a base of not having one of the four basic customer service needs being met.

2. Difficult guests come in many varieties.

3. When difficult guests attack, they usually are not attacking the service provider personally.

4. There are five tips for dealing with difficult guests.

5. The key to achieving quality customer service is to increase the number of service encounter successes and reduce the number of service failures.

STUDY QUESTIONS/DISCUSSION STIMULATORS

1. Why are most difficult customers being difficult?

2. Why shouldn't you take the attacks or challenges from a difficult customer personally?

3. Looking at the five tips for dealing with a difficult guest, what is each tip attempting to accomplish?

4. When dealing with difficult guests, under what circumstances do you, as a service provider, have to cut your losses?

APPLICATION INTERACTION EXERCISE 31

THAT DIFFICULT GUEST

Drawing on the list of differing categories of difficult guests, or adding your own cate-gory of difficult customer, record your ideas of how you could effectively handle that situation.

Difficult Situation _____

What are some things you can do to **not take this situation personally**?

_____

_____

What are some things you can do to **remain calm and listen carefully**?

_____

_____

What are some things you can do to **focus on the problem and not the difficult person**?

_____

_____

What are some things you can do to **reward yourself for handling the situation effectively**?

_____

_____

Under what circumstances would you **ask for help**?

_____

_____

APPLICATION INTERACTION EXERCISE 32

THE CASE OF THE DIFFICULT GUEST

You are working as a guest services associate at the front desk of a large downtown hotel. A middle-aged, well-dressed woman approaches the front desk and asks to see the manager. Your manager is currently out of the area, so you ask if you can be of assistance. She then proceeds to tell you that she is a regular guest at this hotel and that she is very fussy and is used to the best. She doesn't understand why she can't bring her little pet dog into her room and is forced to board her at a local pet motel. She and her little dog have never been separated, and it is completely housebroken and never barks or bites. She hates the thought of her little baby being all alone in this cold and cruel doggy motel that charges her outrageous rates. She goes on and on about how much she loves her dog. Other guests are beginning to line up for your assistance.

How will you respond to her?

Write your response below:

_____

_____

_____

_____

_____

_____

_____

_____

_____

_____

_____

_____

_____

_____

_____

_____

Section IV

SELF-ASSESSMENT—

What Have You Learned?

TEST YOUR KNOWLEDGE—

TRUE-FALSE TEST

_____ 1. Being a customer provides enough experience to fully understand the nature of quality customer service.

_____ 2. Just as long as the customer wins as a result of the service encounter, quality customer service has occurred.

_____ 3. Service can result in a lose-lose situation for both customer and service provider.

_____ 4. Quality customer service is relatively easy to accomplish.

_____ 5. Most important, it takes brains and talent to be successful at delivering quality customer service.

_____ 6. Many current hospitality service providers misunderstand what quality service is all about.

_____ 7. To be successful as a hospitality service provider, one must be open to new experiences and be willing to improve and grow.

_____ 8. The perception of what exactly customer service is may vary from one person to the next depending on life and work experience.

_____ 9. The intangible nature of customer service makes it easier to deal with.

_____ 10. Because customer service is intangible, it is best to allow it to take care of itself.

_____ 11. To say, "The customer is the reason we exist" reflects a customer service perspective.

_____ 12. Adopting a customer service perspective usually results in conducting business as usual.

_____ 13. A service organization cannot be successful unless its service providers are successful.

_____ 14. The term "moment of truth" refers to what happens during a customer service encounter.

_____ 15. External customers do business with you because they have to.

_____ 16. All the various niches within the hospitality industry tend to have the same specific needs, wants, and expectations.

_____ 17. Internal customers rely on others within the operation for goods and services.

_____ 18. Customer service is everybody's job within a hospitality organization.

_____ 19. Providing quality customer service requires a 100 percent success rate.

_____ 20. Quality customer service is fundamentally based on an organization's needs and expectations.

_____ 21. Quality customer service incorporates a system, as well as a human dimension.

_____ 22. "The factory" form of service delivery is often seen in many newly opened hospitality operations.

_____ 23. "The friendly zoo" form of service is skewed toward procedural efficiency.

_____ 24. When asked about service, one of the first thoughts that comes to customers' minds tends to be about timeliness.

_____ 25. Timely service should always include a prompt greeting.

_____ 26. The point of the service encounter when customers tend to be least forgiving is related to postservice timing.

_____ 27. Promptness and timeliness are essentially one and the same.

_____ 28. Timeliness of service and service flow are unrelated.

_____ 29. The nature of service flow is a function of system interdependency.

_____ 30. A balanced system helps maintain service flow.

_____ 31. Because service flow is a total system phenomenon, service providers have very little control over it.

_____ 32. Service flow can be maintained by breaking service into incremental parts.

_____ 33. Knowing in advance the number of customers you will be serving facilitates effective anticipation.

_____ 34. Accurately anticipating hotel occupancy can be a critical service issue.

_____ 35. Anticipation is evident when service is delivered after the guest has requested it.

_____ 36. In hospitality organizations, communication breaks down quite frequently.

_____ 37. The nature of a complete communication exchange facilitates effective communication.

_____ 38. Effective communication occurs when the message received is exactly as it was intended.

_____ 39. Most customers like to complain.

_____ 40. When seeking customer feedback orally, a specific question is better than a general one.

_____ 41. Having one good customer feedback system is usually better than using several approaches.

_____ 42. Being accommodating requires saying "yes" to all customer requests.

_____ 43. Accommodation requires flexible service systems.

_____ 44. When a customer makes a special request, it is easier to say "yes" than it is to say "no."

_____ 45. To one degree or another, all hospitality customers have the four basic customer service needs.

_____ 46. The need to be understood relates primarily to the content of the message and not the emotions involved.

_____ 47. The ability to empathize with a guest increases understanding.

_____ 48. Satisfying a guest's need for comfort relates mostly to physical comfort.

_____ 49. Hospitality guests enjoy feeling important.

_____ 50. Sometimes it becomes necessary to embarrass a customer.

_____ 51. Attitudes often communicate more than words themselves.

_____ 52. The showing of attitudes is an example of a customer service tangible.

_____ 53. Body language refers to nonverbal communication.

_____ 54. Attitudes are conveyed through personal grooming standards.

_____ 55. Sometimes the way words are spoken communicates one's real meaning.

_____ 56. The appropriateness of a particular tone of voice may vary depending on the nature of the hospitality setting.

_____ 57. Attitude metamorphosis is a rare occurrence in the hospitality industry.

_____ 58. Being nice to others requires emotional energy.

_____ 59. It is just as easy to be nice to the last customer of the day as it is to the first.

_____ 60. Contact overload syndrome is a reaction to working in a crowded work-space.

_____ 61. As an attitude catalyst, you can generate either positive or negative attitudes.

_____ 62. Quality hospitality service providers must learn to become their own positive attitude catalyst.

_____ 63. Reflecting a positive attitude is far more important than the actual words spoken during the service encounter.

_____ 64. In most hospitality settings, the use of slang or poor grammar is usually appropriate.

_____ 65. Saying, "please" and "thank you" is always appropriate regardless of the hospitality setting.

_____ 66. Most hospitality customers are called by name during the service encounter.

_____ 67. Having a system of identifying guest names ensures that it will be used.

_____ 68. Most guests do not want their name mentioned during a service encounter.

_____ 69. Attentive service means providing the unexpected.

_____ 70. Being an attentive service provider requires a special skill of being able to tune-in to customer needs.

_____ 71. Reading the guest refers to finding out as much as you can about them before you interact with them.

_____ 72. Rapport involves the emotional relationship between the service provider and the customer.

_____ 73. Rapport can be either positive or negative.

_____ 74. Empathy refers to the ability to walk in another person's shoes.

_____ 75. A customer's age and attire can provide clues to possible services needed.

_____ 76. Groups of customers tend to have differing needs than solo guests.

_____ 77. Being required to sing "Happy Birthday" to all guests celebrating a birthday is an example of service attentiveness.

_____ 78. A result of attentive service would be wowing the guest.

_____ 79. Product knowledge is not really necessary to be able to effectively help the customer.

_____ 80. Most hospitality customers don't need or want assistance from their service providers.

_____ 81. The major problem with all the five forbidden phrases is that they tend to generate a negative relationship with the customer.

_____ 82. Service providers should never reflect hesitation or uncertainty in their responses to customer requests.

_____ 83. To the guest, it is far better to minimize or underestimate the time it may take to deal with a particular service task than to quote an accurate time.

_____ 84. When speaking to a customer, the service provider should avoid beginning a sentence with the word "you."

_____ 85. Rather than tell a customer what you can't do, it is better to relay what you can do.

_____ 86. Sometimes a service provider has to begin a sentence with the word "no."

_____ 87. The purpose of service is to cultivate and accumulate sales.

_____ 88. Hospitality service providers have traditionally been viewed as sales representatives.

_____ 89. As a hospitality service provider, adopting a sales perspective means assuming you can and should sell.

_____ 90. Selling is an extra, added bonus to the job of providing service.

_____ 91. Effective selling requires complete product knowledge.

_____ 92. The four basic customer service needs are unrelated to effectively dealing with customer complaints.

_____ 93. Dealing with customers' emotions is generally not part of a hospitality service provider's job.

_____ 94. When a customer complains, it is more important to deal with it first before apologizing.

_____ 95. To reach agreement with the customer on how to solve a problem or complaint means always agreeing to everything the customer wants.

_____ 96. All complaining customers should be thanked for complaining.

_____ 97. All difficult guests have a complaint of some sort.

_____ 98. One of the hardest customer service skills to learn is not to take attacks from customers personally.

_____ 99. All the difficult guest often needs is some added, extra attention.

_____ 100. Delivering quality customer service requires satisfying all customers all the time.

TEST YOUR SKILL—

SERVICE PROVIDER SELF-ASSESSMENT SCALE

(SPSAS)

Answer each question according to how often you ACTUALLY exhibit the described behavior.

4=Always   **3=Mostly**   **2=Sometimes**   **1=Rarely**   **0=Never**

DO YOU . . .

_____ 1. Consistently provide service in a timely manner consistent with customer needs?

_____ 2. Provide guests, who are waiting for service, with something to occupy their time while waiting?

_____ 3. Keep the sequence of service steps flowing smoothly and incrementally?

_____ 4. Know and deal with customer service needs in order of priority?

_____ 5. Keep one step ahead of customer needs?

_____ 6. Provide needed service to customers before they have to ask for it?

_____ 7. Orally repeat customer orders or requests back to them?

_____ 8. Communicate with fellow team members in a timely, accurate, and thorough manner?

_____ 9. Ask specific questions when seeking feedback from customers?

_____ 10. Provide a mechanism for customer feedback other than an oral response?

_____ 11. Say "yes" to unusual or special customer requests?

_____ 12. Offer a convenience to customers that may be an inconvenience to you?

_____ 13. Work well under minimal or no supervision?

_____ 14. Work in an organized and efficient manner?

_____ 15. Display nothing but positive attitudes on the job?

_____ 16. Provide service with a smile?

_____ 17. Reflect a customer-friendly tone of voice?

_____ 18. Display enthusiasm toward the job?

_____ 19. Use polite and tactful words when speaking to customers?

_____ 20. Avoid using slang or jargon when speaking to customers?

_____ 21. Follow a system that facilitates the use of customer names?

_____ 22. Refer to customers by name when providing or concluding service?

_____ 23. Provide that "extra touch" when servicing customers?

_____ 24. Individualize service to customers when necessary?

_____ 25. Answer all customer questions about products and/or services?

_____ 26. Provide helpful suggestions to customers?

_____ 27. Use effective selling skills?

_____ 28. Mention product and/or service upgrades?

_____ 29. Remain pleasant and calm when customers are upset, angry, or hostile?

_____ 30. Graciously handle complaints to the customers' satisfaction?

S CORING THE SPSAS

In each category, record the number circled for each of the corresponding numbered questions. The resulting percentages will show you your strengths and opportunities for improvement. If you have a lower percentage on a certain skill, that is a good indication that you could benefit from improvement in that area.

EXAMPLE

Timeliness: 1 __**3**__ 2 __**3**__   Total __**6**__ /8 = __**75**__ %

Timeliness: 1 _____ 2 _____   Total _____ /8 = _____%

Incremental Flow: 3 _____ 4 _____   Total _____ /8 = _____%

Anticipation: 5 _____ 6 _____   Total _____ /8 = _____%

Communication: 7 _____ 8 _____   Total _____ /8 = _____%

Customer Feedback: 9 _____ 10 _____   Total _____ /8 = _____%

Accommodation: 11 _____ 12 _____   Total _____ /8 = _____%

Organization/Supervision: 13 _____ 14 _____   Total _____ /8 = _____%

Attitude/Body Language: 15 _____ 16 _____   Total _____ /8 = _____%

Attitude/Tone of Voice: 17 _____ 18 _____   Total _____ /8 = _____%

Tact: 19 _____ 20 _____   Total _____ /8 = _____%

Naming Names: 21 _____ 22 _____   Total _____ /8 = _____%

Attentiveness: 23 _____ 24 _____   Total _____ /8 = _____%

Guidance: 25 _____ 26 _____   Total _____ /8 = _____%

Selling Skills: 27 _____ 28 _____   Total _____ /8 = _____%

Gracious Problem Solving: 29 _____ 30 _____   Total _____ /8 = _____%

Additional Readings

Anderson, Kristin and Ron Zemke. *Delivering Knock Your Socks Off Service*. New York: American Management Association, 1998.

Barlow, Janelle and Dianna Maul. *Emotional Value, Creating Strong Bonds with Your Customers*. San Francisco: Berrett-Koehler Publishers, Inc., 2000.

Bell, Chip. *Customers as Partners, Building Relationships That Last*. San Francisco: Berrett-Koehler Publishers, 1994.

Blanchard, Ken and Sheldon Bowles. *Raving Fans*. New York: William Morrow and Company, Inc., 1993.

Davidoff, Donald M. *Contact: Customer Service in the Hospitality and Tourism Industry*. Upper Saddle River, NJ: Prentice Hall, 1994.

Davidow, William H. and Bro Uttal. *Total Customer Satisfaction, The Ultimate Weapon*. New York: Harper Perennial, 1989.

Ford, Robert and Cherrill Heaton. *Managing the Guest Experience in Hospitality*. Albany, NY: Delmar Thomson Learning, 2000.

Gitomer, Jeffrey. *Customer Satisfaction Is Worthless, Customer Loyalty Is Priceless*. Austin, TX: Bard Press, 1998.

Greiner, Donna and Theodore B. Kinn. *1,001 Ways to Keep Customers Coming Back*. Rocklin, CA: Prima Publishing, 1999.

Griffin, Jill. *Customer Loyalty, How to Earn It, How to Keep It*. San Francisco: Jossey-Bass Publishers, 1995.

Gross, T. Scott. *Positively Outrageous Service*. New York: Warner Books, 1991.

Kandampully, Jay, Connie Mok, and Beverly Sparks, eds. *Service Quality Management in Hospitality, Tourism, and Leisure*. Binghamton, NY: Haworth Press, Inc., 2000.

Karr, Ron and Don Blohowiak. *The Complete Idiot's Guide to Great Customer Service*. New York: Alpha Books, 1997.

LeBoeuf, Michael. *How to Win Customers and Keep Them for Life*. New York: Berkley Books, 1989.

Leland, Karen and Keith Bailey. *Customer Service for Dummies*. Foster City, CA: IDG Books, 1995.

Martin, William B. *The Restaurant Server's Guide to Quality Customer Service*. Menlo Park, CA: Crisp Publications, 1987.

———. *Managing Quality Customer Service*. Menlo Park, CA: Crisp Publications, 1989.

———. *Quality Service, The Restaurant Manager's Bible*, 2nd ed. Ithaca, NY: School of Hotel Administration, Cornell University, 1991.

———. *Quality Customer Service*, 4th ed. Menlo Park, CA: Crisp Publications, 2001.

———. *Quality Service: What Every Hospitality Manager Needs to Know*. Upper Saddle River, NJ: Prentice Hall, 2002.

Michael, Angie. *Best Impressions in Hospitality: Your Professional Image for Excellence*. Albany, NY: Delmar Thomson Learning, 2000.

Nelson, Bob. *1001 Ways to Reward Employees*. New York: Workman Publishing, 1994.

Remarkable Service. Hyde Park, NY: Culinary Institute of America, 2001.

Sanders, Betsy. *Fabled Service, Ordinary Acts, Extraordinary Outcomes*. San Francisco: Jossey-Bass Publishers, 1995.

Willingham, Ron. *Hey, I'm the Customer*. Paramus, NJ: Prentice Hall, 1992.

Index

True-False Test Answers

1. F	26. T	51. T	76. T
2. F	27. F	52. F	77. F
3. T	28. F	53. T	78. T
4. F	29. T	54. T	79. F
5. F	30. T	55. T	80. F
6. T	31. F	56. T	81. T
7. T	32. T	57. F	82. F
8. T	33. T	58. T	83. F
9. F	34. T	59. F	84. T
10. F	35. F	60. F	85. T
11. T	36. T	61. T	86. F
12. F	37. F	62. T	87. T
13. T	38. T	63. F	88. F
14. T	39. F	64. F	89. T
15. F	40. T	65. T	90. F
16. F	41. F	66. F	91. T
17. T	42. F	67. F	92. F
18. T	43. T	68. F	93. F
19. F	44. F	69. T	94. F
20. F	45. T	70. T	95. F
21. T	46. F	71. F	96. T
22. F	47. T	72. T	97. F
23. F	48. F	73. F	98. T
24. T	49. T	74. T	99. T
25. T	50. F	75. T	100. F